3.75

PLANNING
MUSIC
IN THE
EDUCATION
OF
CHILDREN

WADSWORTH MUSIC SERIES

Basic Piano for Adults by Helene Robinson

Basic Resources for Learning Music by Alice Snyder Knuth and William E. Knuth

English Folk Songs: Some Conclusions, 3rd edition, by Cecil J. Sharp (edited by Maud Karpeles)

Five Centuries of Keyboard Music by John Gillespie

Foundations in Music Theory by Leon Dallin

Harmony and Melody, Volumes I and II, by Elie Siegmeister

Help Yourselves to Music by Beatrice P. Krone and Kurt R. Miller

Music Essentials for Classroom Teachers by Robert Pace

Music Fundamentals by Howard A. Murphy with John F. Park

Music in the Education of Children, 2nd edition, by Bessie R. Swanson

Planning for Music in the Education of Children by Bessie R. Swanson

Talking about Concertos by Antony Hopkins

Talking about Symphonies by Antony Hopkins

Teaching Music in the Secondary Schools by Charles R. Hoffer

Toward World Understanding through Song by Robert Nye, Vernice Nye, and Virginia Nye

PLANNING
MUSIC
IN THE
EDUCATION
OF
CHILDREN

A PERSONAL HANDBOOK

BESSIE R. SWANSON

WADSWORTH PUBLISHING COMPANY, INC.
BELMONT, CALIFORNIA

L. C. Cat. Card No.: 65-17774

Printed in the United States of America

TO THE INSTRUCTOR

The wide diversity of skills and interests among your students is probably one of your biggest problems in teaching elementary music education. Some have strong music skills and others have none; some are eager to teach any subject while others are reluctant to teach subjects they have not mastered; some students have excellent potential in both music and teaching itself, but have not grasped the methods of organization so essential to a good teacher. Since no single textbook can meet the needs of all these students, the instructor must help each prospective teacher tailor his music-teaching preparation to his own needs and abilities.

This book contributes an outline of the essentials in elementary music education. The student can use it as a framework for creating a handbook that will serve as a cumulative record of his procedures and materials over his early teaching years. Thus, each student will, in effect, become the author of his own teaching tool.

This project is based on the principles stated in the author's *Music in the Education of Children:*

"Not every classroom teacher is capable of single-handedly providing the rich program of musical experiences his pupils should have. . . . Regardless of who does the major portion of the music teaching, the classroom teacher's interest in music and his skill as a teacher are indispensable to a vital music program in his classroom. Whether he has sufficient musical background and skills to provide *all* the leadership his pupils require, or whether he must call for assistance in specified areas, the responsibility for music in the classroom remains his. He must prepare himself in whatever ways he can to meet this challenge."

The grade level of his teaching interest and the particular skills the student brings to music should be considered in the development of his handbook. An elementary education major should concentrate on plans for use in one or two grades if he is reasonably sure where his first teaching assignment will place him. In many cases, it may be more practical for the student to design broader plans, which later can be adapted to a particular grade.

A major in music might reasonably be expected to develop a very broad teaching handbook. It is probable he will be assigned responsibilities in classroom music for both primary and intermediate grades. In any case, each handbook can be evaluated in terms of (1) how well it reflects the skills and needs of the teacher who will use it, and (2) how well it is adapted to the teaching level for which it is designed.

Two primary considerations in elementary music education form the basis for the organization of this book: (1) musical activities for children, and (2) concepts of music that children learn through their experiences. Activities are outlined in Part 1, because of their importance as the media for musical learning.

Concepts of music are considered in Part 2. For those who are experienced in music, these chapters may serve mainly as a graded check-list of concepts related to each of the elements of music. The grade-level indications should be considered primarily as guidelines for inexperienced teachers, rather than as a fixed grading of any of the concepts. Students who have had limited experience with music may not be able to develop plans for teaching music until they have reviewed these elementary concepts.

Part 1 outlines the important considerations for each of five activities in elementary music education by means of a series of questions. At the beginning of each chapter, page references for Swanson and other pertinent sources are listed. With the aid of these references and others that you may recommend, as well as class lectures and discussions, a student should formulate answers for all the questions. These answers then serve as a basis for his teaching plans. You may wish to specify that some written assignments given at the close of each chapter in the Swanson text be incorporated into the student's handbook as sample teaching materials. In most instances, these rather specific written assignments have not been repeated in this book.

A number of songs, which supplement those available in Swanson and other music education textbooks, are included in the Appendix. They can be used to give the college class practical material to work with when studying elementary music activities and concepts in music. This collection contains songs from various periods of history. It provides some piano accompaniments, which can be useful in the study of harmony and texture in music. Several two- and three-part songs are included, as well as a number of songs that can be accompanied with rhythm instruments, melody and harmony instruments, or bodily movement of various kinds.

Since this is an activities book rather than a teaching-methods book, the songs are printed without comments or directions for use. The student can record his own musical analysis, or describe how the song might be used as a part of the elementary program of musical activities.

This book will help you formulate course examinations in the following ways: (1) Any series of questions selected from Part 1 can be used as the basis for an examination of students' understanding of teaching objectives, procedures, or materials. To limit a question, you may wish to specify its application to a particular grade level. (2) If your philosophy leads you to center more on musical skills and knowledge than on teaching procedures, you can derive an examination based primarily on the concepts of music in Part 2. Two suggested methods are: (1) Play a short recorded composition three or four times at one point in the examination; then ask the students to discuss the essential elements of the music and to list related concepts that children of a specified age could observe and study while hearing and working with the composition. Or (2) hand out copies of a song for the students to analyze from the standpoint of its value in teaching musical concepts in a specified grade.

Regardless of the specific methods you adopt for putting this book to work in your class, its two basic purposes can readily be fulfilled. A personal handbook prepared according to its outline will give a feeling of confidence to the prospective teacher who is just finding his way in music; the future teacher who comes to your class with a good knowledge of music will learn how to organize his knowledge for teaching the elementary pupil.

B. R. S.

CONTENTS

TO THE STUDENT

This book is a framework for you to use in making a personal music-teaching handbook for the elementary grade or grades you hope to teach. The course in elementary music education considers all levels from kindergarten through grade six, because you should be acquainted with the entire field. However, you will be able to make more effective plans for your own teaching if you select a musical repertoire and make teaching notes on procedures particularly applicable to the grade you plan to teach. If there is uncertainty about the grade you should plan for, develop outlines applicable to the two or three grades of your teaching interest (for example, primary, or intermediate, or grades three and four).

Provide yourself with a three-hole, loose-leaf binder for 8½" × 11" paper, the size used here. You can tear sheets out of this book and incorporate them into the binder, which will become your handbook for teaching music. You may wish to use some of the chapter-opening pages as sectional-divider sheets in your handbook. The six sections outlined in Part 1 of this book would make a good organizational structure for your use. You may also wish to incorporate some of Part 2 in a second section of your handbook.

Every chapter of this book provides references to the basic textbook, Swanson's *Music in the Education of Children,* and to other books. The order in which you complete various topics and chapters in your handbook will depend upon the order of reading assignments and lectures given by your instructor.

Interesting musical activities provide the foundation for educating children in music. As an elementary teacher, you should plan for variety and balance in these activities. However, most beginning teachers find their particular skills and background bring success more readily in some musical activities than in others. Tailor a music handbook that will not only help you achieve success and satisfaction in your early teaching, but also help you develop other areas as you grow in confidence and teaching skill. Leave ample room for later additions under all headings. If you plan well, your handbook will serve you for many years as a cumulative record of materials and ideas for teaching music.

The following questionnaire should be filled out and turned in at the second class session. Your answers will help your instructor (1) assess your needs and skills in music, (2) place you with persons of similar interests and needs when classwork is done in small groups, and (3) adapt the course to your individual needs as well as those of the class as a whole.

PERSONAL QUESTIONNAIRE AND
INVENTORY OF MUSIC SKILLS

Name ——————————— Course ——————————— Date ———————

1. College address ——————————————— Phone————————

2. Age ——— 3. College major ——————— 4. Year in college ———

5. High school from which graduated ———————————————

6. What musical instruments have you studied?

    Instrument   Years studied   General proficiency

    a.

    b.

    c.

7. What other musical instruments have you played with some personal satisfaction?

    Instrument   General proficiency

    a.

    b.

8. What singing experience have you had?

    Age or year in school   Situation (chorus, choir, solo, etc.)

    a.

    b.

9. Comment briefly on what you consider to be your singing skills or deficiencies.

10. To what musical programs do you listen regularly? (radio, TV, concerts, etc.)

11. In what musical activities do you now participate?

12. Have you ever been a group leader? (Scout leader, camp counselor, etc.) Explain:

13. Have you had any teaching experience?

    What grade(s)?   How long?

14. What interest or skill have you in the following? (Describe briefly.)
    a. Visual arts

    b. Drama

    c. Dancing

15. What are your plans for teaching?

    a. Grade(s) _____

    b. Subject(s) _____

    c. Other plans _____

PART 1 ACTIVITIES IN MUSIC

It has become accepted practice in elementary schools to teach music through the musical activities of singing, moving to music, playing instruments, listening, and creating and writing music. These are not mutually exclusive, for children frequently sing as they play instruments, and they listen as they participate in other ways. However, such an outline provides a useful means of organization; many music education books and courses of study are set up on this basis, and the first part of this book follows this plan.

As you study musical materials and activities for children, you must also become acquainted with the broader scope of music in elementary education. Chapter 1 in this book calls your attention to questions of integrating music into the classroom.

Chapters 2 through 6 point out the main things a teacher must consider in each of the musical activities and suggest ways of organizing and annotating materials in your teaching handbook. Throughout the reference readings listed within these chapters, the various authors discuss the development of skills (learning to sing and to play instruments, to read and interpret music notation, . . .) and the development of concepts in music (knowledge of rhythm, melody, harmony, . . .).

It will be fairly easy for you to organize within your handbook information relative to the development of music skills. Since the development of concepts is dependent upon the teacher's knowledge of music and his understanding of the learning capacity of his pupils, this is a particular challenge to a beginning teacher. Part Two of this book has been prepared to help you with this important aspect of music teaching. Chapters 7 through 12 contain outlines of the concepts in music that can be derived from experiences with music at all levels.

Notice that the ideas are framed so that they are understandable to children, and notice in what order they are given within each chapter. Although you may have learned music in a different frame of reference, the statements as they are given in these chapters are compatible with the idea of learning music through meaningful experiences. Throughout the activities chapters of this book you will find repeated reference to the musical concepts in Part Two. Study these listings carefully and find out how to integrate this essential learning with the musical activities you organize for your pupils.

chapter 1　The Scope of Music in the Elementary Classroom

The values of music

Music's relationship to the other arts

Relating music to science, mathematics, and physical education

The relationship of music to the social studies

Contributions of music to living today

Evaluating pupil-progress in music

Evaluating the teacher's musical potential

Preparing teaching plans

The first chapter of your personalized handbook for music should establish the cornerstones for your teaching. Although these may be the last entries you make in your book, the topics involve questions that will require some reflection on your part. Therefore, we pose them first. You can search for answers in the references and in your experience with music education throughout the course.

In the curriculum for music, the teacher is concerned with the inter-relationship of musical activities for children and musical concepts developed from those activities. But music also has relationships with other subjects such as science, social studies, and the other arts. The classroom teacher is the guardian and promoter of the interrelations within the total curriculum designed for the child.

The elementary teacher often relates music and the social studies in his planning. He helps children learn folk songs of their own and other countries, thus helping them to share the feelings of others and to become aware of the music of other cultures in the world. These studies are important and you should give them consideration. In addition, you should recognize the significant part music plays in contemporary social living; greater understanding and appreciation of this role can be developed within the elementary school music program.

The questions that follow will help you prepare statements and outlines to form a framework for your music program. Work out the answers to these problems at any time during the course that the lectures and reading assignments provide you with the necessary resources.

1. What Are the Values of Music to Education and Living Today?

Music has had a regular place in elementary education in the United States since the early 1800s, and generally throughout history in other lands. What values make music so important to education and to human life? As a teacher, you should have concern for music in the curriculum. Perhaps your own experience has provided you with ample conviction on the subject, and all you need do is plan how to state this conviction effectively. Such a statement would be appropriate in this chapter of your personal handbook for teaching music.

Your textbook has some answers to this question, and may provide guidelines for your study (Swanson, pp. 1–5). Edman, the philosopher, is concerned with the question in his *Arts and the Man;* Chapters 2 and 5 in particular are recommended. Broudy considers the question from the point of view of a philosopher of education. Some very practical answers are supplied by Mursell in Chapter 1 of *Music and the Classroom Teacher.* For complete information on these and other reference books turn to the bibliography.

2. How Does Music Relate and Contribute to the Other Arts?

The Greek definition of music included all arts over which the Muses presided, and this broader definition can be useful to a general teacher. Beginning with an impression in any art medium (poem, picture, story, music), one can find some means of expressing a similar feeling in another medium, or find a work of art in another medium that has a related expression. You might work with other members of your class to find some good examples of such interrelationships that would be useful at the grade level of your interest. Consider the visual and language arts, the dance, or creative dramatics.

Art subjects should be taught so that they induce feeling—whether feeling in response to another's art expression, or feeling expressed through the child's artistic enterprise. The arts provide effective, socially acceptable ways of expressing feeling that often people are afraid to reveal. This is one reason it is important for civilized people to develop functional skills in the arts. The general teacher is in the fortunate position of being able to use any art media to help children find freedom of expression or to reinforce experiences in one media with related experiences in another.

You will find that many of the examples given in the discussion of bodily movement and music in Swanson, Chapter 3, can easily be expanded to include related expression in language arts and visual arts. Other examples, with some suggestions for the use of art with music, are shown on pp. 228–235.

3. How Can Music Enter into the Study of Science, Mathematics, and Physical Education?

A study of the scientific principles of tone production and resonance can be part of elementary projects in science at different grade levels. The children can investigate the different ways tone is produced; they should consider the source of tone (the vibrating object) and the amplifier of the tone (the resonating body). After children learn these principles and relate them to the several kinds of musical instruments, they can begin to understand why an instrument produces a tone with particular characteristics of loudness and timbre.

Music has been associated with mathematics and astronomy since the days of Aristotle, but not because of its rhythmic aspect—

that two quarter notes equal a half note, and so on. Rhythm is too flexible to be arithmetic; we work with duple, triple, and quadruple beats and divisions of the beat, but from the point of view of flowing muscular response (physical education) rather than as arithmetical concepts. Rather, music is associated with mathematics through the relationships of tones to each other. The octave is the basis for the division of tones into musical scales. When children of the intermediate grades learn intervals (the octave, fifth, fourth, third, etc.), they begin to work with the harmonic series in music, the real basis of a relationship between music and mathematics. Some simple science exhibits show how a vibrating string is divided into partials. At this level, however, we usually do not try to show how the ancients arrived at the harmonic series.

You will find many useful relationships between physical education and music, particularly the rhythmic aspect of music. Study the physical education activities recommended for the grade of your interest and list suggestions on how a more extensive use of music could help to make dances and other forms of movement more rhythmic, and hence more valuable in the development of grace, poise, and health.

Decide to what extent a study of sound can be incorporated in the science projects recommended for the grade you hope to teach. What relationships can be drawn between the scientific studies and musical tone? Include in your teaching handbook suggestions and lists of source readings that will be helpful to you. Some basic music series have units on the science of sound, and these library books for children will be useful in the classroom: Kettlekamp, *Magic of Sound* and *Singing Strings* (Morrow); Berger and Clark, *Science and Music* (McGraw-Hill); Pine and Levine, *Sounds All Around* (McGraw-Hill).

4. How Can Music Be Related to the Social Studies?

At every grade level there are opportunities to use music within the framework of the social studies to help children expand their cultural horizons and better understand people everywhere. Swanson, pp. 253–258, and 39–40, provides some insight into the question. You will need to find out what social-studies topics are considered at the grade level of your interest. Begin by making a sample outline of the most important musical considerations within a selected topic. Find out what criteria you will need for judging whether a particular song or recorded composition is a good representative of the culture to be studied.

Elliott, Part 2, Chapters 9–14, lists many materials for the study of music in relation to successive periods in American history; Tooze and Krone discuss music as a resource for social studies. Nye and Nye, Chapter 11, give sample units that may be of interest to classroom teachers. Myers, Chapter 12, states the characteristics of music in different cultures and countries, and lists many recordings of ethnic music.

5. How Can I Help Children Become Aware of the Contributions of Music to Their Lives?

Probably the most significant observation to be made under this heading is that people in our culture take music for granted because there is so much of it. We turn the dial for relaxing music to accompany freeway driving, newspaper reading, or a nap; we sit at the piano or pick up a guitar to idle away a few moments, improvising or playing familiar songs. Music accompanies our religious celebrations, our recreation, our socializing, and our advertising, often unnoticed. How can you teach children to use music more effectively for their own benefit?

Children study primitive and foreign cultures and find that there is music of one kind or another for ceremonies, for dancing, and for the individual expression of feeling. Human beings throughout history have found in music and the other arts a necessary fulfillment of aesthetic needs, and all these uses of music carry over into our own culture. Your studies related to the value of music and the social-studies relationships of music provide you with some background for an answer to the present question.

6. How Should I Evaluate Pupil-Progress in Music?

Teachers are charged with responsibility for evaluating and grading pupil-progress in music, as in most subject areas. So, during this course you should give some thought to the problem of grading. Helpful discussions will be found in Swanson, pp. 260–261; Jones, pp. 351–354; and Nye and Nye, pp. 362–368.

Prepare a statement on Evaluation in Music to be included in this chapter of your music handbook. What does a teacher need to consider when he establishes grades for music at the teaching level you have selected? The school may have a policy that makes grading in music mandatory; in what ways might you meet the requirement?

7. What Is My Potential for Teaching Music?

In the first six grades, the classroom teacher often instructs his class in music; sometimes a special teacher does so, but frequently the two work together. You will find this topic discussed in Swanson, pp. 12–14. It is safe to say that almost every classroom teacher will need to assume some responsibility for music in his classroom. The handbook you compile for this course should reflect your potential as a music teacher: If you have vocal limitations, you will plan to use recordings of songs to supplement your voice; you may find it necessary to concentrate your teaching preparation in other areas such as listening, social studies, or science correlations. The quality of your handbook could be evaluated in terms of how well it will meet your needs as a teacher.

Throughout the course in elementary music education, you will be testing your abilities and growing in experience and musical skill; what can you expect of yourself as a beginning teacher of music? Have you abilities you can develop further during the first few years of teaching? What parts of the music program can you deal with competently alone?—with some help from a special teacher or supervisor? Prepare an evaluation of yourself in respect to the teaching skills needed for the various aspects of the music program; include this evaluation in the first chapter of your handbook.

8. How Can I Prepare to Make Effective Schedules and Plans?

Music is more than a subject for study; it is also an activity for pleasure and recreation in the elementary classroom. Every teacher should consider how music in both of these roles can be incorporated into the daily schedule. Plans will vary with the grade level and the assignment of teaching responsibility; if you are able to assume most of the responsibility for teaching music in your classroom, you will have many choices in your planning (see Swanson, pp. 22–28, and 143–145).

If you have less music-teaching skill, you may be assisted by a special teacher whose schedule will be a prime, but presently unknown, factor in your plan. However, you will still have responsibility for coordinating music with other subjects, and using it as a pleasurable, informal activity for your class. Under this heading in your handbook, include notes to help you in such planning during your early teaching. Further suggestions will be found in Nye and Nye, pp. 57–63.

Music activities and lessons also need planning. Any lesson should have variety and balance of activities and learning; there should be continuity from one lesson to another. Although some planning must be delayed until you are acquainted with the children of your class, it will be useful to have two or three sample plans for music lessons at your class level. One might center on a single musical activity, showing how different compositions can be studied; another might center on a particular element of music and the ways various activities can be used to illuminate it.

Since plans of this kind depend upon the teacher's knowledge of the subject matter, it will take some time to prepare your response to this question. When your handbook is near completion, you will find you have a great deal of material to use. Planning a lesson will involve selecting the topic and musical material from your collection, then deciding upon the musical activities for the children and the musical skills and concepts you hope to teach. If your lesson is built around a new song, the planning suggestions outlined in Swanson, p. 219, may be helpful.

chapter 2   Singing

The singing voices of children

Organizing singing activities

Teaching materials available

The repertoire of songs

How children learn songs

Improving singing skills

Teaching music through singing

Music was predominantly a vocal activity when it first came into the American elementary curriculum, and today people tend to identify classroom music with singing. Many of the basic series music books still are primarily song books, and in spite of the diversity of activities in music education, singing remains important from many points of view.

You will find that most children like to sing and expect to in school; they also want to learn—how to sing and how to play instruments, and about the nature of music itself. For many years music teachers have given careful attention to the problems related to singing; there are many sources of information in the field. In this chapter, seven important questions form the basis for your studies of this topic. Your basic resource will be Swanson, Chapters 2 and 6; Chapter 7, pp. 191–210; and Appendix B, pp. 276–278. Since your instructor will assign the readings in a sequence that supports his presentation of the material in the course, you may be able to answer some of these questions sooner than others. All elementary grades are considered in the textbook, so you must take care to include in your handbook only the recommendations that are suitable for children of your chosen grade or grades.

Other good references are: Pitts, et al., pp. viii–xi, for a valuable discussion on children's voices; Sheehy, Chapter 4, for helpful ideas about songs for children, and Seeger, pp. 33–48, which is especially helpful to those concerned with teaching songs to younger children.

1. What Do I Need to Know about the Singing Voices of Children?

The singing of children should be easy and natural without strain or artificiality. You will need to understand the essential characteristics of your pupils' voices so you will feel as confident in guiding their singing voices as in working with their speaking voices.

Consider quality as well as range, and observe that the singing voice is produced by the same flexible physical mechanism that produces the speaking and "playground" voice. Find out what differences might be expected between voices of primary pupils and those of intermediate children.

2. How Can I Organize and Facilitate Singing Activities?

A music program should offer different kinds of opportunities for singing at various grade levels. Singing is not always a formal, full-group activity; some objectives can be achieved more effectively in small groups. Singing is not always teacher-directed; while making music, children can develop skills in leadership as well as musicianship. They sing in assemblies, in selected choirs, and on the playground, to name only a few singing situations.

As a prospective teacher you should concentrate now on the recommendations of others for singing activities which will bring you and the children immediate success and pleasure. Your long-range goal should be a diversified singing program that enables every child to develop his own particular musical talents.

3. What Teaching Materials Are Available for Singing?

There is a wealth of song literature and it is a considerable task to evaluate it in terms of the singing needs of children. Generally speaking, this is the responsibility of a music specialist; it is he who must choose music for the elementary choirs and serve as chairman of the committee selecting basic or supplementary song books for classroom use. The classroom teacher's responsibility is to acquaint himself with the basic music series and supplementary materials supplied by the school district.

Your instructor can tell you which basic music series is used in your state or county and should receive most of your attention. A second basic series often is used as a supplementary text; single, specialized books and records provide further variety. Listings of these materials are available in the references (especially Swanson, pp. 276–278, and Sheehy, pp. 75–77). Your teaching handbook should include suggestions of books and records that will be useful to you.

4. What Repertoire of Songs Should Be Used?

The repertoire of songs you select for your class should be appealing, varied, and of good musical quality. For many teachers, the basic series book provided by the school district serves as the chief source of song material. However, no single book can supply all the songs a particular group of children will need during a school year; it is always necessary to expand the repertoire in certain directions by drawing on supplementary sources. An important purpose of your personal teaching handbook is to furnish an accumulative record of the materials you find useful in teaching.

You should first of all determine what types of songs should be sung by children of your teaching level. The table of contents and the classified index of the basic music series offer such information, and the references for this chapter also suggest desirable types and topics for songs at various levels.

After you have a general acquaintance

with the available song books, and after you know what song topics will be useful, compile a representative group of songs that are appealing and of good musical quality. If you have not developed the necessary discrimination for quality in songs, a discussion of "What is a Good Song?" (Swanson, pp. 28–30) may be helpful; also, sing and discuss the songs with other members of the music education class.

A separate page in your teaching handbook should be prepared for each topic that will be useful at the teaching level you have selected. This is only the beginning of an annotated collection; therefore one or two good titles under each heading will be sufficient at this time. The right-hand column of the page should be reserved for teaching notes. Keep these brief, noting only a reminder of the character of the song and its possible use. During your teaching, you will find this column very useful, so leave ample space for additional comments.

Example 1 shows a form that has proved useful. Notice that the source of the song is given in a short code, followed by the page number. The key and first tone of the song should be indicated in another column, so that after you have memorized the song you can refer to the key without having the song book. The third item shows how you can indicate a minor key. The tune-up code gives the pitch to be sounded on pitch pipe or piano (the major-scale key note) and the scale number or syllable on which the song begins. This system is explained in Swanson, pp. 148–153. There are other approaches to the minor mode however; you should seek the advice of your instructor on this point, using whatever system seems most useful. The important thing is to adopt some practical method of tuning each song and use that method consistently. If the song as written seems too high, indicate a transposition, as shown in the tune-up column for the first entry of Example 1.

Star those songs you consider essential heritage songs for children in your community. Within your teaching notes include tone calls and tonal patterns that are important in the study of a particular song (see Swanson, pp. 167–169, 204–206).

5. How Do Children Learn Songs at This Grade Level?

Individuals of any age learn songs either by hearing them sung or by reading notation on the printed page. In the early years children learn entirely by listening; gradually they learn symbols and the learning process becomes that of interpreting printed symbols. Most song learning in elementary grades is a combination of these two approaches.

Many teaching techniques are employed to help children learn songs, while helping them grow in musical independence through the use of music notation. Swanson, pp. 153–166, describes how the teacher's singing voice, recordings of other voices, and classroom music books can be used to help children learn songs. From this and other sources, collect information that will be helpful to you. References to other teaching techniques and ways of learning songs by playing various instruments are cited in Chapter 4.

6. How Can Children's Singing Skills Be Improved?

Every class has children with wide variations of singing skills. As the teacher of a particular grade, you must evaluate abilities and help each child improve during his year with you. Probably no one will dispute the desirability of an adequate singing voice, but some people question the possibility of helping each child develop such a voice. Generally, the problem is not insurmountable; but it does call for understanding and ade-

EXAMPLE 1

ART SONGS *

TITLE	SOURCE	TUNE-UP	TEACHING NOTES
"Cradle Song"	GwM V-19 (see also page 85 this book)	E♭ ⌈mi ⌊do transp. C —do	Art song in 2 parts; chiefly 3rds in harmony. See *Harmony* A-5 Well-balanced form in 4-meas. phrases. See *Form* A-2, 6, 7 Up-beats to all patterns; varied cadences. See *Melody* A-4, 5; B-4, 5; C-5.

HAWAIIAN SONGS *

TITLE	SOURCE	TUNE-UP	TEACHING NOTES
"Aloha Oe"	Bir VI-120 (see also page 91 this book)	F ⌈mi ⌊<u>so</u>	See *Melody & Harmony Instruments.* In 2 parts with melody in lower voice.

SPECIAL DAYS—HALLOWEEN *

TITLE	SOURCE	TUNE-UP	TEACHING NOTES
"Shadow March" (Rowley)	Foll VI-22 (see also page 86 this book)	B♭ —la (g minor)	Mysterious, Halloween-type song by 20th Cent. composer. Recorded; Teacher's Ed. suggests rhy. instr. acc. See *Rhythm* B-8, 9, 10; D-5, 6. Use of chromatic scale. See *Melody* D-3, 5.

* In your teaching handbook these topics would occur on separate pages.

quate teaching skills at the primary level. A few problem voices may be encountered in the intermediate grades where strengthening of singing skills means developing abilities to sing harmony parts and to sing with greater expressiveness. The references for this chapter, especially Swanson, pp. 166–178 and Pitts, pp. viii–xi, will help you answer this question.

7. How Can Musical Skills and Knowledge Be Developed through Singing?

In the references for this chapter, you are advised to select songs with affective appeal, or those that appeal to children through the activity they suggest or through association with things children like. These are the first considerations in the selection of song literature. However, you also have the responsibility of helping children develop skills and knowledge of music through the songs they sing. It requires more skill to select appealing musical literature and then find ways to teach music concepts from experiences with it, than to outline the concepts first and then select musical examples that will facilitate the learning. However, the effective teacher of music as an expressive medium will always give prior consideration to the quality and appeal of the music.

Some songs you select may lend themselves to the study of rhythm through the use of rhythm instruments or expressive bodily movement. Others may offer good opportunities for the use of various melody or harmony instruments. Songs such as these should be cross-filed in your handbook under later chapters dealing with particular activities.

The predominantly vocal ways of promoting an understanding of melody and pitch involve the use of sol-fa syllables and scale numbers. After consulting the references for an explanation of these techniques, you should make an outline of the ones that are applicable to the grade level or levels you have chosen. Follow the same procedure in formulating the ways children can learn about phrasing and musical form, harmony and texture, tone, color, and style in music. The references for this chapter, especially Swanson, pp. 191–210, provide analyses of teaching techniques that can be used in the study of all of these elements. Decide which songs in the repertoire you have selected can be used to bring certain musical concepts, as outlined in Part Two, to the attention of your pupils. Make appropriate references as shown in the sample entries, Example 1.

chapter 3   Moving to Music

Purposes and values

Organizing the activities

Movement and rhythm

Movement related to melody and form

Songs for interpretation

Instrumental compositions for interpretation

Bodily movement is used in music education to help children discover music. Through expressive movement, they learn rhythm, line, phrasing, and dynamics, all basic to music. Movement itself is not only an art form in the dance, but also a natural childhood activity that can be developed and refined for greater expressiveness through physical education and creative dramatics.

Most music education textbooks give some consideration to the use of bodily movement in the study of rhythm; some authors go further and suggest ways movement can be used to help children understand melodic line, phrasing, cadence, and form in music. All are aspects of music that children should study; and expressive movement has a place in teaching plans at every grade level.

This chapter poses six questions on the use of bodily movement, designed to help you develop Chapter 3 in your music handbook. Your basic reference for this study will be Swanson, Chapter 3. Notice, however, that the author draws bodily movement into other activities as they are discussed throughout the book, as in listening activities, pp. 225–226 and 230–235; in Elements of Rhythm, pp. 80–90; even in Management of the Singing Situation, pp. 153–160 and 179–183.

Sheehy, Chapters 7 and 8, discusses the broad, creative ways movement and dance are used. Andrews' entire book is important to the elementary classroom teacher because it relates music and rhythm to creative dramatics. Check the table of contents for topics particularly applicable to the questions in this chapter. Orff shows how clapping, patting the knees, and stamping can be used in techniques designed for children of various ages, pp. 66–75 and 80–87.

1. What Are the Purposes and Values of Movement as a Musical Activity?

The value a teacher gives to a procedure usually determines how much he will use it in the classroom. If you are kinesthetically oriented, you will readily understand why childhood specialists consider bodily movement important in education. However, if your response to music has been primarily intellectual, you should observe children using bodily movement in music or creative dramatics to get some idea of the expressive values.

Throughout the references for this chapter you will find statements on the value of expressive bodily movement in music education. Some consideration should be given the relationship between bodily movement as an activity in music and bodily movement in physical education, in creative dramatics, and in dancing. The immediate objectives for the use of movement in these areas differ, although some of the same materials and procedures may be used. A teacher who would help children use movement effectively in these various activities must discriminate among the objectives.

2. How Can I Organize and Facilitate the Use of Bodily Movement?

In your reference reading, you will find practical suggestions for classroom planning and management in the use of bodily movement. Singing, listening, and the playing of instruments are activities used in connection with bodily movement at all levels. Look for suggestions on how these activities can be interrelated at the grade level of your choice.

Give special attention to the procedures outlined. Success in handling this ac-

tivity may depend upon appropriate space for movement, effective musical accompaniments, or pupil management. Both creative freedom and social control are necessary. Different procedures usually are recommended for different age groups; special planning is often needed for children who have limited experience and confidence in the use of bodily movement as an expressive medium. Make a brief outline of procedures you feel will be important at the grade level you have selected.

3. In What Ways Can Movement Be Used to Help Children Understand Rhythm?

Development of rhythmic awareness in young children should grow out of rhythmic play activities. Primary teachers should consider how music can be related to natural locomotor and axial body movements. Older children, as well as younger children, should use large body movements and dancing in their study of rhythm.

A learning program stressing creativity in movement as well as in playing instruments will offer children opportunities to create rhythm with bodily movement and then develop simple instrumental accompaniments for the movement. The rhythmic movement, then, is not interpretive, but creative in itself; the necessity of providing an accompaniment offers valuable opportunities for the development of further insights into rhythm. After studying the references given in Chapter 4, you will understand how accompaniments can be created. Then, you can make cross-references in your handbook, to relate the playing of instruments to bodily movement.

More precise movements such as clapping, patting the knees, swinging the arms in time-keeping movements, marking time with the feet, and moving in various dancing patterns are activities helpful in the study of rhythm at all elementary levels. Outline the ways these and other kinds of movement can be used at the grade level of your choice.

In your reading, you will find references to specific aspects of rhythm that can be experienced and studied through the use of bodily movement. These aspects of rhythm are listed under the first three headings in Chapter 7.

4. How Can Movement Enhance Understanding of Melody and Musical Form?

Studies of melody and musical form often are carried out in conjunction with activities used for the study of rhythm. Frequently such strong rhythmic music as marches and folk dances give children opportunities to interpret and study melody and structural design. Many of the more varied and creative movements used for characterization and dramatization take their cues from melodic movement and structure of the music, as well as rhythm.

After studying about movement activities that can aid in the study of melody and musical form, outline these activities under this heading in your handbook. Some generalizations on melody in the first two sections of Chapter 8, Part Two, can be interpreted through movement. The first three sections of Chapter 11 on form and design in music list concepts that can be shown in children's interpretive dramatizations and dance patterns.

5. What Songs Lend Themselves to Interpretation through Bodily Movement?

You now should be able to view the repertoire of songs for your chosen grade level and decide which ones would lend themselves to bodily movement. Consider the several types of movement that can be used and plan for variety. It would be advisable for you to select one song as an example under each type of bodily movement (see especially Swanson, pp. 45–47 and 64–70). Write brief notes about the possibilities you see for the use of movement within the song. Follow the format shown in Example 2, giving the song's title, source, and tune-up, and reserve the right hand side of the page for teaching notes.

Determine how the use of movement can help children understand the various aspects of rhythm, melody, and form that are outstanding characteristics of the song. Specify what generalizations outlined in Part Two could be pointed up as a result of the activities you recommend.

Cite other songs that might be treated in similar ways and make cross-references to songs that are listed in your music-teaching handbook in other chapters.

6. What Instrumental Compositions Can Be Interpreted through Bodily Movement?

In references, you will find suggestions of instrumental music that can be studied through the use of expressive bodily movement. Some are compositions a teacher might play on the piano; many recorded instrumental pieces also are recommended (see Swanson, pp. 49–54, 57–64). Frequently, the appropriate grade levels for particular music are indicated to guide inexperienced teachers. However, you should realize this is not a fixed grading. Also, you will find many compositions suggested in later references to listening activities that are adaptable to the use of bodily movement (see especially, Teacher's Guides for R.C.A. ADVENTURES IN MUSIC SERIES). Therefore, you should plan

EXAMPLE 2

INTERPRETATION THROUGH MOVEMENT

TITLE	SOURCE	TUNE-UP	TEACHING NOTES
"Who Will Come with Me?"	MfL 1-9 (see also page 94 this book)	F—mi transp. D—mi	Trad. skipping or marching song. Accompany with rhy. instr. on duple beat and melody rhythm. May clap, mark time, hop.
"The Green Dress"	Bir III-28 (see also page 95 this book)	G—<u>so</u>	See rhythm instr. acc. Duple meter, shown in rhythmic walking or clapping.
"Ah, Lovely Meadows"	NMH VI-168 (see also page 96 this book)	B♭ $\begin{cases} \text{so} \\ \text{mi} \end{cases}$	Czech Folk Song; march or schottische. Regular quadruple meter, begins on down beats, slight syncopation. *Form:* stanza & refrain with clear balanced phrases, each 4 meas. long. Harmony in lower voice in 3rds & 6ths.
"Shoo Fly"	MM II-82 (see also page 97 this book)	F—mi	American game song; simple circle dance shown in Teacher's Edition. *Rhythm:* mild syncopation in 1st meas. followed by uneven division of beat in 2nd meas.

to make cross-references to activities in Chapter 3 when you are assembling Chapter 5 of your handbook.

Select instrumental compositions that can serve as examples under each different kind of movement (e.g. fundamental movements, characterizations and drama, marches, dances, etc.). Teaching notes for each should include references to aspects of rhythm, melody, or form that can be expressed. Be sure to note the complete title, composer, and type of source (book or record) so you can find it when it is needed. If only one part of the composition is to be used, specify exactly which part.

You should listen to the music you use in teaching notes. Teaching suggestions in books or other publications can be of great help, but you must adapt them for your own use; sometimes this means expanding the material, but often it means selecting only the information appropriate to your grade.

chapter 4   Playing Instruments

RHYTHM INSTRUMENTS

Quality and types of instruments

Organization and classroom use

Uses with songs

Uses with instrumental compositions

MELODY AND HARMONY INSTRUMENTS

Types to be used

The study of melody

The study of harmony

The special instrumental program

Many different kinds of simple instruments are used in classrooms at all grade levels, and many aspects of music are involved under this heading. It is suggested that you explore single-toned percussion instruments (rhythm instruments) in the first half of Chapter 4 of your handbook. In the second part, you will consider melody and harmony instruments.

All instruments should be played rhythmically whether alone or in ensemble. As an elementary teacher you should encourage the natural development of a sense of rhythm—first through bodily movement, then through the sounding of rhythm instruments as the children move and sing, and later through rhythm ensembles. Children with rhythmic responses developed this way find greater challenge in playing tuned instruments rhythmically. This is an important developmental sequence; look for it in your study of the recommended readings for this chapter.

A. Rhythm Instruments

Single-toned percussion instruments, which should be used at all grade levels, are as valuable for the quality of their sounds as for their instrumental simplicity.

They are used in much folk music as well as in the symphony orchestra. The rhythm instruments of the primary grades are simple adaptations of percussion instruments adults use in more sophisticated music.

Since the rhythm instruments are so easy to play, children can use them early to sound rhythm patterns, metric beats, and accents. Gradually they learn how these aspects of rhythm are shown in notation. Your basic reference for this topic is Swanson, Chapter 4; you will also find suggestions for the use of rhythm instruments in Chapter 3, pp. 47–48. Sheehy, pp. 78–99, describes creative ways of using the instruments.

1. What Quality and Types of Rhythm Instruments Are Recommended?

One of the important uses of single-pitch percussion instruments is for developing concepts of instrumental tone color. Children should be led to discover that the instruments may be played in more than one way for different tonal sound effects. Later they will learn how to classify tone in terms of duration, pitch, quality, and loudness (see Swanson, p. 78). All instruments are classified and used by the composer in terms of these characteristics. Find out how an understanding of the varied qualities of sound in the orchestral instruments (see Part Two, Chapter 10) can grow out of early experiences with rhythm instruments.

Some schools have ample quantities of instruments on hand. In others you may have to order what you will need, or even help your pupils build or repair their instruments. Search out information for your handbook to prepare yourself for these eventualities.

2. How Can I Organize and Facilitate the Classroom Use of Rhythm Instruments?

One of the early uses a teacher makes of rhythm instruments is to play them and have children play them, in accompaniment with rhythmic movement. Different rates of speed, different rhythm patterns, and variety in tone quality are necessary in the accompaniment of different kinds of movement (see Swanson, pp. 47–48). Your experience and observations in the college class can give you an idea of the accompaniment possibilities of these instruments.

You should consider establishing a "music corner" in your classroom as a place for instrument storage and for pupil-exploration of the instruments themselves. Individuals and small groups of children use rhythm instruments in various creative ways. They tap out rhythm patterns inherent in names and other speech patterns, and create accompaniments for chants and rhymes. Older children use instruments with contrasting tones in improvisatory rhythm ensembles. Find out what a teacher can do to foster and guide such activities. The recommended references for this chapter will provide you with most of the information you will need. Include in your teaching-handbook samples of this type of work that might be expected at the grade level at which you plan to teach.

3. How Can Rhythm Instruments Be Used with Songs?

There are certain fundamental ways a teacher can use rhythm instruments to aid children's study of rhythm and musical form. If you know what concepts need to be developed (see the outline of concepts in Chapters 7 and 11 of Part Two) you will more readily understand the purpose behind the procedures recommended.

Find songs to serve as examples of different ways in which rhythm instruments can be used in accompaniments (Swanson, pp. 78–87, 90–92). When carefully developed, such accompaniments also highlight certain characteristics of rhythm and form in the song. Example 3 shows brief notes on songs suitable for different grade levels.

Folk songs of different countries use various kinds of rhythm instruments. You should find out what instruments can be used authentically with the music of countries your class may study (Myers, Chapter 12),

and you should be acquainted with typical rhythm patterns for different kinds of dances (Swanson, pp. 66–68). Include in your handbook examples and brief notes on any techniques that may be useful for your grade.

4. How Can Rhythm Instruments Be Used with Recorded Instrumental Compositions?

Single rhythm instruments can be used to accompany recorded music with selected rhythm patterns; ensembles of rhythm instruments can be used to play student-created orchestrations. Participation in these activities will lead children into interesting studies of rhythm, tone color, form, and style in music. You will need to find out how rhythm instruments can be used to point up these elements of music and what compositions are best for demonstrating the various elements. Older children will be able to go deeper into the study of all the elements of music than younger children (see Swanson, pp. 92–98).

Selections by composers of traditional European music can be used as a basis for rhythm orchestrations. In addition, some recorded music of foreign and primitive cultures might be used in this way. In this chapter of your handbook, prepare some examples of various useful procedures. Include additional titles of compositions you might work out in similar ways at a later date.

B. Melody and Harmony Instruments

In the elementary school, tuned instruments include those in which different lengths of wood or metal are struck to produce specified pitches; those in which strings of different lengths are sounded (including the piano and stringed instruments of the orchestra); and various wind instruments. An extensive program for teaching children to play instruments and to understand musical concepts is possible with the aid of these instruments.

Children can begin to observe characteristics of melody as early as kindergarten and the first grade when they play xylophones and "song

EXAMPLE 3

RHYTHM INSTRUMENT ACCOMPANIMENTS

TITLE	SOURCE	TUNE-UP	TEACHING NOTES
"M'sieu Bainjo"	Foll V-52 (see also page 93 this book)	F—so	Rhythmic folk song with syncopated div. of beat. See *Rhythm* B-1, 3–7. Use rhy. instr. to contrast melody rhy. with metric beat; use rhy. of 1st 2 meas. as continuous acc. pattern. Regular alternation of I & V₇ chords. See *Harmony* B-2.
"Carmen, Carmela"	Ginn VI-62 (see also page 92 this book)	G—<u>so</u>	Mexican folk song harmonized with 6ths and 3rds below melody. I & V₇ chords only. $\frac{2}{4}$ meter with triplet division of beat. Extended upbeats throughout. Maracas play contin. patt. of triplet & two 8th notes throughout.
"The Green Dress"	Bir III-28 (see also page 95 this book)	G—<u>so</u>	So. African song. Lively rhythm in cut time with evenly div. beats. Play 2 beats per meas. on rhy. sticks, melody rhy. on chop sticks, accent on drum. See mv't. activities. *Form:* 4-meas. phrases with change in last part of phrase (a–a'–b–b). Use of sequence.

bells." In addition to receiving pleasure from sounding the instruments, children will begin to investigate pitch from an objective point of view. In the second, third, and fourth grades, the piano and recorder or "song flute" can be introduced as boys and girls learn melody construction and relate pitch to staff notation.

At the intermediate grade level, as children increase their knowledge of melody, they can begin to learn how tones are combined to make harmony. Under the guidance of special teachers, they also begin learning to play standard orchestral instruments and soon combine these skills with other classroom music activities.

Most children are eager to play melody and harmony instruments; if you can incorporate these instruments into classroom music activities, you will greatly enhance the value of the music program. Your basic reference, Swanson, in Chapter 5, details teaching techniques on the use of melody instruments and on the introduction of harmony by means of the autoharp. Sheehy, pp. 95–142, suggests approaches to the piano and other melody instruments of particular interest to teachers of younger children. Nye and Nye, Chapter 5, give attention to piano chording, show pictures of various instruments, and provide useful listings of songs to be accompanied by classroom instruments.

1. What Melody and Harmony Instruments Should Be Used?

Among the melody instruments used in elementary music education are the multi-toned percussion instruments of the glockenspiel and xylophone types. These instruments are related to the multi-toned percussion instruments of the orchestra. You will need to learn what are the attributes of the various kinds of instruments that have been adapted for children, and what use is made of them at the various grade levels.

The autoharp is an important stringed chording instrument in the elementary music program. Other chording instruments children play are the guitar, the ukulele, and the piano. Among the useful wind instruments are the plastic song flute and the wooden flute, called a recorder. The references for this chapter tell you how to use these instruments in the classroom.

Include in your teaching handbook necessary descriptions, brand names, and sources for the instruments you will be able to use in your teaching. You may wish to write to instrument companies for brochures or visit a music store to obtain current price lists and addresses.

2. How Can Tuned Instruments Be Used in the Study of Melody?

In general, all types of classroom melody and harmony instruments are used at all grade levels. However, their musical purpose in the classroom and the extent of their use become broader as children advance to the intermediate grades. Younger children may use only a limited number of tones of a melody instrument, and their teacher guides them in the activity. At the intermediate level, children become increasingly proficient, playing in different keys and learning multiple parts; individual children assume leadership in group music-making.

The references cited for this topic give adequate procedures and examples on how

EXAMPLE 4

TUNED INSTRUMENT ACCOMPANIMENTS

TITLE	SOURCE	TUNE-UP	TEACHING NOTES
"The Bell Doth Toll"	Ginn VI-199 (see also page 90 this book)	F—so	Three-part round; harmony recurs: I—‖I—‖I V‖I :‖ Play: root tones of chords; any line repeatedly.
"The Sheep-Shearing"	Bir IV-76 (see also page 89 this book)	G—so transp. F—so	English folk song, smooth & melismatic; triple meter. *Harmony:* I—IV—V₇ chords on autoharp or res. bells. Good contrast between chordwise & scalewise melody.
"Little David Play on Your Harp"	MfL IV-29 (see also page 94 this book)	F—mi	Spiritual; pentatonic scale. *Rhythm:* duple meter with up-beat patterns & syncopation. Play drone on accent; rhythmic, 2-beat ostinato using xylophone; clapping or claves on off-beats.
"Aloha Oe"	Bir VI-120 (see also page 91 this book)	F⌐mi ⌐so	Hawaiian song, 2-part harm. with melody in lower voice. *Harmony:* I—IV—V₇ chords for ukelele or autoharp. *Form:* Stanza & refrain, each 8 meas., antecedent & consequent phrases, 2 meas. long.

the various instruments can be used with songs. Considering your grade level of interest, select a song that will serve as a suitable example for each procedure you find described. Arrange pages in your handbook for teaching notes you prepare, using the format recommended in Chapter 2. List other songs that might be used in similar ways.

Pleasure and the development of skills in playing the instruments are both important objectives; but you must also give constant consideration to teaching the basic principles of melody. Suggestions are incorporated in the discussion of procedures in the recommended references. The musical concepts are summarized and graded in Chapter 8 of this book.

3. How Can Tuned Instruments Be Used in a Study of Harmony?

The autoharp is the easiest instrument children and teachers can learn to play for song accompaniments; it frequently is played by all children in the fourth grade, and sometimes by those in the primary grades. Simplified piano accompaniments using two chords can be learned by third graders. Children in the intermediate grades make wider use of the piano. Select songs appropriate for your teaching level that can be accompanied in the simple ways described in the references; list them in your handbook using the format shown in Example 4.

Teaching techniques utilizing these instruments have been developed so that chil-

dren learn simple principles of harmony in the intermediate grades (see Swanson, pp. 128–139). Chapter 9 of this book outlines music concepts that are learned through experiences with these instruments. In listing songs with tuned instrument accompaniments, add teaching notes to show what concepts of harmony might be learned with a particular song.

4. How Can the Classroom Music Program Be Coordinated with the Special Instrumental Program?

The piano can be used by children both as a melody instrument and as a chording instrument. The references offer many suggestions on how it can be used in simple ways by children at different grade levels. A child who has learned to play the piano or other instrument should be encouraged by using his skill in the classroom music activities. In this, and in other ways, the classroom teacher can lend support to the special instrumental music program (see Swanson, pp. 126–127).

Orchestral instruments such as violins and cellos can be used in simple ways by all children in the intermediate grades. Suggestions for playing easy harmony parts with them are given in the references. Children who have developed some skill in these and other orchestral instruments can handle the the more difficult harmony parts in music books.

chapter 5   Listening to Music

Informal listening

The repertoire for study

Concert opportunities

Listening to music permeates all the other musical activities, but it also can be a central activity in itself. Because listening is a major form of musical enjoyment in adult life, it is doubly important that children learn to listen attentively to music. With the excellent recordings available, you should have no difficulty finding good music for classroom listening. In addition to older collections, there are two relatively new record libraries, ADVENTURES IN MUSIC by R.C.A. Victor, and the BOWMAR ORCHESTRAL LIBRARY, that have been planned especially for use in elementary schools; both contain helpful teaching notes for each composition (see Swanson, Appendix B, pp. 278–283).

When an experienced listener hears music he continually draws upon his understanding of music concepts as listed in Part Two of this book. The references give suggestions on how children can learn to listen to music in this way, as well as in terms of its programmatic content and the sheer pleasure in its sound.

The basic reference for this chapter is Swanson, Chapter 8, but Chapters 3 and 4 also give suggestions applicable to the program in music listening. For an orientation in "The Role of Listening" you should read Hartshorn. McMillan, Chapter 5, outlines many "Listening Adventures" that are immediately useful, and Sheehy, Chapters 9 and 10, suggests broader, more varied resources.

1. In What Informal Ways Can Recorded Music Be Used in a Classroom?

You will find that listening to music in the elementary classroom does not always occur in a group listening lesson. If it is desirable for children to know and love certain music, they must have many opportunities to hear it. Your reading resources suggest some ways in which the entire class, as a group and as individuals, can be given more extended, informal opportunities for listening (Swanson, pp. 222–228, and Taylor). You may wish to list recommended compositions for such general listening at the grade level of your interest.

Although physical response to music through bodily movement and the playing of rhythm instruments has received attention in previous chapters, you may wish to make cross-references to these activities under listening. Children also find satisfaction interpreting music through verbalization (discussion and story-telling) and the use of other art media. Although it should not always be necessary for children to interpret music by means of an activity, such responses can be helpful when children are learning to listen and to respond with sensitivity.

2. What Criteria Should Be Considered in Selecting Titles of Music for Study?

After becoming acquainted with the references, you may wish to establish an outline of the listening repertoire for your particular grade under headings such as:

a. *descriptive compositions,*
b. *music of a particular composer or style,*
c. *music in a particular form, or*
d. *music featuring particular voices or instruments.*

For one composition under each heading, prepare teaching notes that would enable you to guide children's listening without further research on your part. With each composition, you should decide what characteristics of the elements of music are readily heard and should be drawn to the attention of the children.

In the study of tone quality of instruments and voices you should become acquainted with the characteristics of instruments as listed in Chapter 10. Decide what recorded compositions could be used to help children at your teaching level know tone color, and list books for children's research on the subject; many materials of this type are listed in the references for this chapter.

3. What Kinds of Concert Opportunities and Listening Projects Should Be Encouraged?

Children have opportunities to hear good music in school or community concerts and on TV, radio, and recordings at home. The interest a teacher shows in these activities often greatly influences children's attitudes toward such opportunities for listening to music. Make a few notes about the ways in which you can direct children's interest in out-of-school listening of various kinds. What kind of children's concerts might be planned as a result of school-community cooperation?

You should give some consideration to how music listening can be made part of the educational trend toward enriching opportunities for study by individual pupils. Find out how headsets can be used for individual and small-group listening projects in your classroom, and what library books on music are available to give individuals freedom to learn at their own pace. All of these topics are discussed in the references for this chapter.

Adequate equipment and materials are

essential for satisfying listening in the classroom; if you were asked by your school to order a record player or other equipment for music listening in the classroom, would you know what to recommend? Where would you find the necessary information?

chapter 6   Creating and Writing Music

Creating songs in a group

Individual improvisation and melody-writing

Creating accompaniments

In a broad sense, all musical activities offer opportunities for creativity, but creativity in music also can be very specific and personal. The natural tendencies of children to wonder, to readjust and rearrange, and to explore any available media lead them to make up sound effects, chants and rhythms, and original tunes.

While developing this chapter of your music-teaching handbook, you should reconsider creative opportunities that have been brought to your attention in connection with musical activities outlined in other chapters: Chapter 3, Question 3; Chapter 4A, Question 2; Chapter 4B, Question 2; and Chapter 5, Question 1. Make any cross-references that may be necessary to provide you with adequate understanding of materials and procedures for exploiting creative opportunities.

In the references you will find further suggestions for developing creativity in music at the grade level of your choice. Give particular attention to the projects for both individuals and groups suggested by the questions in this chapter.

The basic reference is Swanson, pp. 6–7, 117–124, 210–219. You will find examples of children's original songs and descriptions about group song- and poetry-writing in Dykema-Cundiff, pp. 218–232; Myers, pp. 140–152; and Nye and Nye, pp. 276–289. Coleman, Chapters 8, 10, and 11, describes an even greater variety of musical composition by individual children.

1. What Kinds of Group Creativity of Songs Can Be Carried Out?

Traditional manifestations of creativity in the elementary school are original verses and original melodies composed by an entire class. You will find suggestions for (1) creating new words for selected melodies, and (2) creating melodies for selected poems; sometimes both melody and text are original. Following the procedures for group creation of songs that you find recommended in your reading: (1) write an original melody for a selected poem; (2) create a new verse for any easy melody you find appealing.

Include these original works as samples in your music handbook. Write them in staff notation as well as in some kind of simplified notation. Make notes on the procedures you should follow in undertaking projects of this kind in your classroom.

2. What Opportunities Can Be Made to Help Individual Children Improvise and Write Music?

Children can use any of the melody instruments for improvising tunes. They play for pleasure in the sound and in the activity itself. Such spontaneous tune-making is valuable, and teachers should encourage children at all grade levels to engage in it. You will find procedures telling how to begin by using only a few tones of the scale and move up to melodies using the pentatonic scale, and eventually the diatonic scale (see Swanson, pp. 117–120). With the necessary equipment, boys and girls in the second grade are able to notate their own songs.

Using the five tones of any pentatonic scale, create a melody for a nursery rhyme. Include this as a sample in your teaching handbook and make brief notes on procedures recommended to help you provide these and other kinds of creative opportunities for members of your classroom.

3. How Can Children Create Accompaniments for Pentatonic Songs and Rounds?

Going beyond single melodies, there are procedures whereby pupils from the third grade upward learn to create two and three different parts for an instrumental ensemble or song accompaniment (see Swanson, pp. 120–124). Listen to some of the easier accompaniments provided on the recording and shown in the book by Carl Orff. This will give you a broader understanding of how rhythmic clapping, drones, and ostinati can be used with pentatonic songs.

Add a two- or three-part accompaniment to your original pentatonic song; then include notes in your teaching handbook that will enable you to guide children in making their own original accompaniments. Creative activities such as this give children first-hand experience with the elements of music. It is impossible to estimate the importance of such opportunities for some individuals in your class.

PART 2   CONCEPTS IN MUSIC

The curriculum in music for children in the elementary school is planned for (1) the development of skills in musical activities, and (2) the development of understanding about music itself. As a teacher you need to know how children grow in their understanding of the elements of music and principles of its construction. Part Two is devoted to outlines of concepts in music that children can acquire as a result of musical experiences up through the sixth grade.

All of the concepts are stated in terms of generalizations of what is heard (the aural). A marginal notation indicates the grade level at which the idea might first be encountered. All of the statements listed are valid at the level indicated, and in grades above. But remember, they should be viewed with reference to a musical setting. Throughout your readings in music education you will find it repeated that children develop deeper musical understanding and better skills as they progress through the elementary grades. Mursell * states it this way:

"What our understanding of growth and development clearly seems to imply is a *cyclical* sequence or order of topics. . . . Items that need to be presented do not occur once for all at some predetermined time. They appear again and again, always in new settings, always with added meanings."

In observing the grading of the generalizations on the following pages, keep in mind that what may be introduced in a setting and on a level appropriate for second graders must be pointed out again to older pupils for broader as well as more precise application in different musical contexts. Some of the musical qualities listed may seem so simple and obvious that you wonder why they have been included. This author has found that an inexperienced teacher may block his own effectiveness as a teacher because he does not understand that what is obvious to him may not even be noticed by his pupils. You are urged to give attention to the way adult statements of the concepts are cut down to child-size portions.

At the end of some of the following sections, notation for the elements of music is outlined in tables that could be useful as charts in a

---

* James L. Mursell, "Growth Processes in Music Education," p. 157, Chapter VI, from Nelson B. Henry, Ed., *Basic Concepts in Music Education.*

classroom. The teacher should use notation (the visual representation of music) whenever he feels it can help children better understand the musical effects they are hearing, singing, or playing. Some notation is useful at the second grade level, but much more use should be made of it at the sixth grade level. The various music education methods books provide adequate guidance on this subject.

Music is an art; therefore it often does not conform to descriptions that we establish in efforts to organize and learn about it. Every musical composition is unique in some respect; once we establish some reasonable generalizations we can observe in what ways a particular composition adheres to or deviates from the usual in its characteristics of rhythm, melody, or form. Under each heading in the following chapters you should:

1. make your own notes for clarification.
2. cite musical material in which you find a particular generalization well exemplified.
3. add to or break down the generalizations as you find necessary at the grade level with which you are concerned.

Some of this work will be done during your studies in music education; however, further clarification and examples will arise in the course of your own teaching, so leave space for later additions. You may wish to tear out these pages and incorporate them in your music-teaching handbook in a way that will be practical for continued work with the subject matter.

One skill you should develop is the ability to analyze songs and other music to find out what qualities are noticeable in each. The following resources will be helpful:

1. The compositions your instructor may use in class to give you experience with music and to show you how such analysis is done. (Musical examples in the Appendix of this book can be used in this way.)
2. Teachers' manuals for the graded music series which analyze the song material and point out important characteristics in each composition. Look for this feature in the graded series you expect to use.
3. Notes for teachers that analyze recorded instrumental music in the educational-record libraries for elementary schools (see R.C.A. Victor, Adventures in Music and the Bowmar Orchestral Library).
4. Musical examples in your music education textbook where various aspects of the music are analyzed and related to activities at the elementary level.
5. Other specialized publications in music education, containing numerous compositions from the common elementary school repertoire, showing how the music can be analyzed and studied within the framework of the musical activities. You will find examples for every grade in these sources (see Bergethon and Boardman, Schubert and Wood).

As you become more competent in dealing with music and understand this approach to music education, you will find your own music handbook most useful for recording what you want to remember about each composition.

chapter 7

Characteristics of Rhythm

Pace and character of movement

Rhythmic motive or pattern

Beat, meter, and accent

Rhythm patterns related to meter

Notation for rhythm

One of children's first ideas about rhythm comes as a general awareness of its pace and character: that it can move fast or slow, and that it can be characterized as graceful, majestic, heavy, or nimble.

The smallest rhythmic unit is the motive, defined as a grouping of one or more unaccented tones in relation to an accented one. In elementary education the use of the term "rhythm pattern" is preferred because it sometimes may be a larger unit than the musician's concept of "motive." In children's musical studies, music is analyzed in terms of its meaningful parts; there should be no attempt to dissect it at the technical level of a music theorist. Hence, a rhythm pattern that has meaning and unity for a child may be identical with the theorist's rhythmic motive, or it may consist of more than one motive. In later studies these patterns can be seen as groups in larger, interrelated units that comprise the musical phrase.

After learning the general characteristics of rhythm and the way it falls into patterns, children are ready to study the different organizations of beats that underlie rhythm in music. The teacher's first responsibility is to expose his pupils to rhythm patterns in various meters and to point out the relationship between the underlying beat and the rhythm.

Later, when children see notation in their song books, they can begin to learn the accepted terms and the meanings of notation for rhythm. The subjective terminology that expresses what one hears and feels in rhythm is used so that learning notation will be merely a matter of attaching symbols to something already familiar. Visual examples of these should be used where possible when discussing concepts of rhythm, as outlined in the following pages. The symbols used to indicate rhythm in the printed music score are also given in this chapter.

Of course, rhythm does not exist by itself in music; it is affected by other elements of music in various subtle ways. If you as the teacher know what is meant by the following characteristics of rhythm, you will be able to follow this outline in teaching concepts of rhythm effectively. You must draw upon your own experiences with rhythm in music and dancing, but some of these references may help you better understand what you have experienced: Boyden, pp. 10–18, Copland, pp. 33–48, Mursell (II), pp. 253–279, Ratner, pp. 28–41.

A. Pace and Character of Movement

1. Music can move fast or it can move slowly. (Later, pace in music is referred to as *tempo*.)
2. Some fast music may be light; other fast music may seem heavy and vigorous in movement.
3. Slow music may seem calm and quiet, or it may be ponderous and heavy.
4. Some music has a steady, even movement like running or walking, but other music may have a steady but uneven short-long movement, like galloping or jumping.
5. One piece of music can be played or sung at faster or slower speeds, arousing different feelings at each different speed.
6. Usually the rhythm of one piece of music moves at the same speed throughout, but sometimes it may slow down gradually near the end or at some place in the middle. (Later this effect is identified as a *retard*.)
7. Sometimes the rhythm of one part of a composition is speeded up gradually, often to make up for a previous slowing down. (Later this effect is called *accelerando*.)

first grade upward

8. Sometimes only the melody is accelerated or slowed, while the accompaniment keeps a steady pace. (Later this effect is identified as *rubato*.)
9. Different speeds and qualities of movement in music are designated by certain English and Italian terms:

grave—slow, solemn	*allegretto*—moderately fast
largo—very slow and broad	*animato*—animated
lento—slow	*allegro*—quick, lively
adagio—leisurely	*vivace*—brisk, fast
andante—moderate and flowing	*presto*—very fast
cantabile—in a singing manner	*leggiero*—light, graceful
dolce—sweetly	*maestoso*—majestic
grazioso—gracefully	*molto*—very much
moderato—moderate	*poco*—a little

fifth grade upward

10. A moderate tempo is about the speed of a heart beat (72 pulses per minute). Sometimes the composer specifies the tempo as a certain number of beats per minute.

sixth grade upward

B. Rhythmic Motive or Pattern

1. Rhythm in music consists of groups of rhythm patterns; the tones in some rhythm patterns are regular and even, but in other patterns some tones are short and some are long.

second grade upward

2. A rhythm pattern may consist of tones that are long and slow-moving; a piece with rhythm patterns like this can be restful and quiet, reverent and solemn, etc.

3. A rhythm pattern may consist of tones that are short and are played or sung fast; a piece with rhythm patterns like this can be brilliant and exciting, lively and dancing, etc.

second grade upward

4. A rhythm pattern usually can be played by itself as a satisfactory repeated figure; sometimes the syllables and words in a song help determine the length of a rhythm pattern.

5. One tone in a rhythm pattern usually seems heavier than other tones; the heavier tone often is the second or third, but sometimes it is the first or last tone in the pattern.

6. When the tones of a rhythm pattern are regular and even, the effect is less exciting than one in which the tones are more irregular in length and occurrence.

7. A rhythm pattern may be repeated once or several times in one composition; and it usually is alternated with other patterns.

third grade upward

8. Two short rhythm patterns may be grouped together to form a longer pattern; sometimes only part of the pattern is repeated.

fourth grade upward

9. Rhythm patterns within a phrase may be even in number, symmetrical, and balanced; sometimes an imbalanced, unsymmetrical effect is desired so the rhythm patterns are designed to help achieve this effect.

10. A rhythmic motive (rhythm pattern) can be varied (developed) in a number of ways: it may be lengthened (extended), or shortened (fragmented), played twice as fast, or played half as fast, etc.

fifth grade upward

C. Beat, Meter, and Accent

1. The beat is regular and continuous throughout most pieces of music. Particularly in marches and dances, the beat is felt strongly as a framework for the rhythm patterns in the music.

2. Lullabies and other gentle pieces have an underlying beat but in these it is much more subtle.

first grade upward

3. The beat must be set at a suitable speed (tempo) for each piece; it can vary considerably from one composition to another, but it should always be a comfortable speed for beating time. (Later this can be seen as one reason for different meters, e.g. $\frac{2}{4}$, $\frac{2}{2}$, ¢ , or $\frac{2}{8}$.)

4. When beats are grouped in units of two the music is said to be in *duple meter*. This can be the meter for a march or a dancing song and it is sounded: *one-two, one-two.* (Later it can be shown that $\frac{2}{4}$, $\frac{2}{8}$, fast $\frac{2}{2}$, ¢ , and fast $\frac{6}{8}$ represent duple meter.)

second grade upward

Notation for Rhythm

Notes and Rests

whole note	𝅝	𝄻	whole rest
half notes	𝅗𝅥 𝅗𝅥	𝅗𝅥 ▬	half note and half rest
quarter notes	♩ ♩ ♩ ♩	♩ 𝄾 ♩ 𝄾	quarter note and quarter rest
dotted half note and quarter note	𝅗𝅥. ♩	♩ ▬.	quarter note and dotted half rest
eighth notes	♫ ♫ ♬	♪𝄾 ♪𝄾 ♪𝄾 ♪𝄾	eighth notes and eighth rests
quarter and eighth notes showing syncopation	♪ ♩ ♪ ♪ ♩ ♪	𝄾 ♩ 𝄾 ♩	quarter notes on off-beats
dotted quarter notes and eighth notes	♩. ♪ ♩. ♪	♪ 𝄾. ♪ 𝄾.	eighth notes and dotted quarter rests
sixteenth notes	𝅘𝅥𝅯𝅘𝅥𝅯𝅘𝅥𝅯𝅘𝅥𝅯 𝅘𝅥𝅯𝅘𝅥𝅯𝅘𝅥𝅯𝅘𝅥𝅯	♪. 𝄾♪ 𝄾♪. 𝄾♪ 𝄾♪ 𝄿	dotted eighth notes and sixteenth rests
dotted eighth and sixteenth notes	♪. 𝅘𝅥𝅯 ♪. 𝅘𝅥𝅯 ♪. 𝅘𝅥𝅯 ♪. 𝅘𝅥𝅯	♪𝄿. ♪𝄿. ♪𝄿. ♪𝄿.	sixteenth notes and dotted eighth rests

Through the placement of symbols, this chart shows the
related time values of different kinds of notes and rests.

Eighth notes and sixteenth notes are shown in two forms:
with cross beams and with separate flags.

5. When beats are grouped in units of three the music is said to be in *triple meter*. This can be the meter for a waltz or a minuet, and it is sounded *one-two-three, one-two-three*. (Later it can be shown that $\frac{3}{4}$, $\frac{3}{8}$, fast $\frac{3}{2}$ and fast $\frac{9}{8}$ represent triple meter.)

6. In any meter the first beat is slightly stronger than the other beats in the group and it is called the *accent*. (Later the use of measure bars to mark off accents and metric units can be shown.) — *second grade upward*

7. In *quadruple meter* the beats are grouped in fours with an accent on the first beat and a lesser accent on the third beat. (Later $\frac{4}{4}$, C, $\frac{4}{8}$, fast $\frac{4}{2}$, and fast $\frac{12}{8}$ can be shown to represent quadruple meter.) — *third grade upward*

8. A slow duple meter that has a swing is counted in six beats: *one-two-three, four-five-six*. In this meter there is an accent on the first beat and a lesser accent on the fourth beat. ($\frac{6}{8}$ and $\frac{6}{4}$ can be shown to represent this slow *compound-duple meter*; $\frac{9}{8}$ similarly represents *compound-triple meter*.) — *fourth grade upward*

9. In some folk and contemporary music unusual meters containing groupings of five or seven beats are encountered. In such meters the beat is steady, but the occurrence of the accent on an odd numbered beat gives an unsymmetric rhythmic effect. (Meters such as $\frac{5}{4}$ and $\frac{7}{4}$ can be shown to give this effect.)

10. When the beat continues at a steady pace throughout a composition while the meter changes so that the accent is shifted, an exciting, unsymmetrical rhythm is achieved. This effect is found in some folk dances and contemporary music. — *sixth grade upward*

D. Rhythm Patterns Related to Meter

1. A rhythm pattern can have a smooth but square-cut movement when its tones flow evenly, twice as fast as the beat. (Later various patterns of even quarter, eighth, and sixteenth notes in $\frac{2}{4}$, $\frac{3}{4}$, and $\frac{4}{4}$ meter can be shown to have these characteristics.)

2. A rhythm pattern can give a feeling of roundness and flow when the tones of the pattern divide the beat into three parts. Many nursery rhymes have rhythm patterns of this kind. (Later various eighth, quarter, and dotted-quarter note patterns in $\frac{6}{8}$, $\frac{9}{8}$, or $\frac{12}{8}$ can be shown to have these characteristics.) — *second grade upward*

3. A rhythm pattern may have tones that move exactly with the beat; in other patterns, some tones may move half as fast as the beat, and they can be combined with faster and even slower tones. (Gradually various combinations of quarter, half, dotted half, and whole notes can be seen.)

4. A rhythm pattern may not take up all of the beats in a meter; sometimes the pattern is repeated, another is sounded, or there is a period of silence called a *rest*. — *third grade upward*

Common Metric Units

(showing meter signatures and some measure bars)

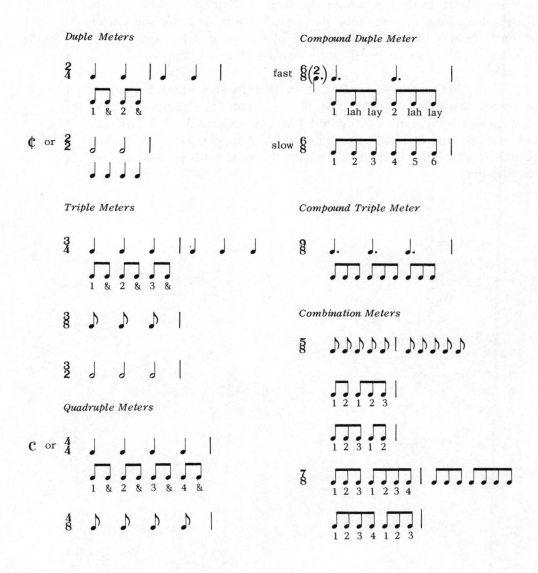

5. Occasionally a rhythm pattern begins with its most important tone on the first beat of the meter, but in many other rhythm patterns one, two, or three quick light tones precede the most important tone. Such short tones leading to the accent are said to be on the *up-beat*. (Later it can be shown how rhythm patterns with up-beats cut across measure bars.)

6. Many rhythm patterns have tones that divide the beat unevenly. A common pattern is that in which the beat is divided into four parts with the long tone getting three parts of the beat, and the short tone one part. (Later various combinations of dotted quarter and eighth or dotted eighth and sixteenth notes can be shown to represent such patterns.)

fourth grade upward

7. When a rhythm pattern is arranged so that its important tone does not coincide with the strong beat in the meter, the pattern is said to be *syncopated*. Many syncopated Latin American rhythm patterns have a short tone on the beat, followed by a longer tone on the unaccented part of the beat, or a rest on the beat with tones sounded after the beat.

fifth grade upward

chapter 8   Characteristics of
                               Melody

Melody as a complete unit

Melodic motives

Melodic intervals

The organization of tones within scales

Notation for pitch

Melody in some music seems to be the most obvious expressive element, and in many songs it is essentially the whole effect. Children's first study of melody should be in terms of its expressive qualities. Only after considerable experience with complete melodies and the component parts, phrases and motives, should children be concerned with melody in terms of intervals and scale relationships.

On the following pages are listed the qualities of melody that are revealed in the experiences children have with melody in singing, playing, and listening activities. With adjustable glockenspiels, resonator bells, and piano keyboards readily available, children can learn these essentials of melody by direct experience with them. Such an approach is supported by this outline because the analysis of intervals and the organization of scales is explored completely without reference to notation. Because notation for pitch is important, it is included in this chapter but the teacher must use his own judgment about when the children are ready for a visual representation. Studies of your music education textbook will provide adequate guidance on this subject.

The musicianship of the teacher and the quality of the musical material used largely determine how soon children learn to recognize the expressive qualities of melody. As early as the first and second grade, children can notice the rise and fall of the melody line and observe its natural division into phrases. Second grade children also can begin to sense the influence of a scale system upon a melody; they will notice that a melody stopping on a certain tone (the tonic) has more feeling of repose than a melody that stops on another tone.

The motive is the shortest self-contained, expressive fragment of melody. The melodic motive is called a tonal pattern in primary-level music education, for the same general reasons that the rhythmic motive is called a rhythm pattern in the early grades; the use of the term "motive" can be initiated at about the fifth grade level. In the primary grades, tonal patterns are used in teaching songs and training voices. (See references to tonal patterns and tone calls, Swanson, pp. 167–169 and 204–206.) Children should become aware of differences in length of tones and melodic direction in the pattern. In the intermediate grades children begin to be aware of the interrelationships of melodic motives in a phrase. At about the fifth grade level the teacher can begin to refer to the difference in pitch between two tones as an interval.

College students who need to increase their own understanding of melody will find these references helpful: Boyden, pp. 21–33, Copland, pp. 49–60, Ratner, pp. 15–28. Songs included at the back of this book exemplify various aspects of melody.

A. Melody as a Complete Unit

1. A melody may rise, it may fall, or it may stay generally on one level.
2. In rising or falling, a melody can move smoothly by scale steps (*conjunct*), or it can move abruptly by large steps (*disjunct*).
3. The tones of a melody may seem to flow in one long continuous line, or they may be shaped into small groups (*motives*).

> *first grade upward*

4. Certain tones in every melody are restful, but other tones seem restless and tend to move to a restful tone. The home tone (*the tonic*) is the most restful tone.
5. A melody may have two or more parts (*phrases*) that are set off by halfway stopping places (*cadences*).

> *second grade upward*

6. Melodies usually have a high point (*climax*); some melodies rise directly to the high point, but others rise gradually through several levels.
7. The mood and feeling a melody arouses is determined to some extent by the way it moves. A melody that remains near one level, using *repeated tones* and *neighboring tones*, can seem calm and restful. Lullabies have this characteristic.
8. Some melodies sound unusual because they use only five different tones. (Later these may be identified as melodies written in the *pentatonic* scale).
9. Some melodies have a slightly different, darker sound than others; they are said to be in the *minor mode*, whereas the brighter sounding melodies are in the *major mode*. (Later this can be explained as the result of lowering the third and sixth degrees of the major scale.)

> *third grade upward*

10. Scalewise movement in a melody can suggest strength if it rises steadily; relaxation if it falls. A melody that moves up or down by large steps may suggest boldness.
11. A melody may have tones that are both quite high and quite low in pitch; such a melody commands attention and is said to have a wide *range*.
12. A melody that moves through the tones of a chord is said to move "chordwise." Much folk music is organized around chord tones.

> *fourth grade upward*

13. A melody often has a framework of essential tones that is filled in by other tones.
14. In many songs each syllable in the word is given one tone, but in some music one syllable is given several tones. (Later these two types of melody may be identified as *syllabic* and *melismatic*.)
15. Sometimes many words are sung or recited on just a few tones. This is characteristic of *recitative* used in opera or oratorio for the narrative parts of the text.

> *fifth grade upward*

B.   Melodic Motives (Tonal Patterns)

1. Some tonal patterns are longer than others; some are as short as two tones, others may be six or seven tones in length. — *first grade upward*

2. A tonal pattern may consist of a few tones moving one step at a time up or down the scale; these are called *scalewise* patterns.

3. A tonal pattern may consist of a few tones that are far apart—that is, going from low-to-high, or high-to-low in a wide leap.

4. A tonal pattern may consist of the tones of a chord (e.g., *do-mi-so*); many folk songs have *chordwise* patterns in the melody. — *second grade upward*

5. A longer tonal pattern may consist of both scalewise and chordwise movement among the tones (e.g., *so-la-so-mi*).

6. Some tones within a pattern may be *repeated tones;* others may be *neighboring tones* (e.g., *so-so-mi; so-la-so-mi*).

7. Rhythm is part of the tonal pattern; if the tones remain the same but the rhythm changes, the pattern is different.

8. In a motive (tonal pattern), one tone usually is more important than the others; this important tone may be in the middle of the pattern, at the beginning, or at the end.

9. Within a melody, a motive can be repeated exactly, or it can be changed (varied) the second or third time it is used. — *fourth grade upward*

10. When a motive is repeated, but on a higher or lower level, the repetition is said to be *in sequence.*

11. Sometimes two adjacent motives are quite different from each other; they are said to *contrast.*

12. A melodic motive can be changed (*developed*) in a number of ways: it may be lengthened (*extended*), or shortened (*fragmented*), changed in rhythm, turned upside down (*inverted*), and so on. — *fifth grade upward*

C.   Melodic Intervals

1. The distance from low *do* (1) to high *do* (8) is a very wide leap. (Later it can be shown that by counting the beginning and the ending scale steps and all the steps between, there are eight tones in this interval, called an *octave.*)

2. The distance from *do* (1) up to *re* (2), and the distance from *re* (2) up to *mi* (3) is one step; it is a small interval. (Later identified as a *major second.*) — *second grade upward*

3. The distance from *do* (1) up to *mi* (3) is an easy skip; it is the first part of the tonic chord and is used for tuning-up to sing. (Later identified as a *major third.*)

Organization of Scales

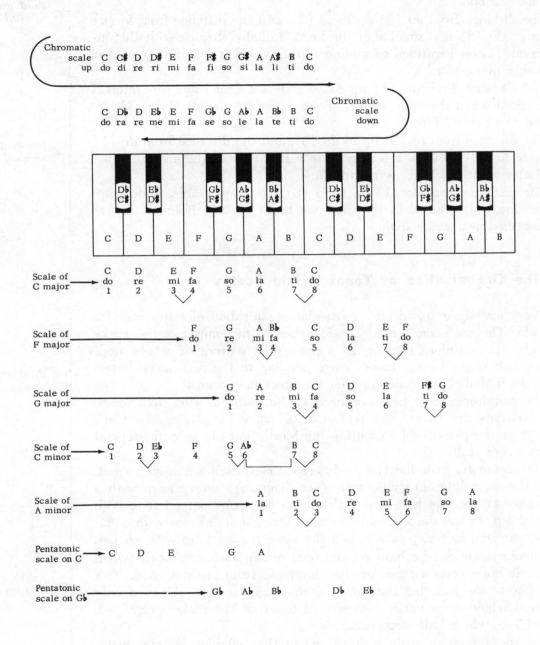

4. The distance from *mi* (3) up to *fa* (4), and the distance from *ti* (7) up to *do* (8) is a half step; this is a very small, tight interval. (Later identified as a *minor second,* which is one half step smaller than a *major second.*)

5. The distance from *mi* (3) up to *so* (5), and the distance from *la* (6) up to *do* (8) is a small skip; Brahms' "Lullaby" begins with this interval. (Later identified as a *minor third,* which is a half step smaller than a major third.)

third grade upward

6. The distance from *do* (1) up to *so* (5) is a firm leap; this interval is heard when the open strings of the violin are tuned. (Later identified as a *perfect fifth.*)

7. The distance from *so* (5) up to *do* (8), and the distance from *do* (1) up to *fa* (4) is a leap; this interval is heard at the beginning of "Taps." (Later identified as a *perfect fourth.*)

8. The distance from *do* (1) up to *la* (6) is a comfortable, wide leap; this interval is heard in the first two tones of "My Bonnie." (Later identified as a *major sixth.*)

fourth grade upward

D. The Organization of Tones within Scales

1. Every melody is based on a particular organization of tones called a scale. The scale most used for melodies in our music is the *major scale:* seven different tones, in a prescribed pattern of whole steps and half steps, having names corresponding to the first seven letters of the alphabet. (See diagram on the preceding page.)

2. The pentatonic scale has been used as the basis for some folk songs; it has only five tones. This scale can be made by playing the black keys on the piano, or by omitting the fourth and the seventh steps of any major scale.

third grade upward

3. The chromatic scale has twelve different tones, each a half step apart. In the ascending chromatic scale (see diagram), tones shown with a sharp (♯) are one half step higher than the same named tone with no sharp. In the descending chromatic scale, tones shown with a flat (♭) are one half step lower than the same named tone with no flat.

4. A major scale can be built on any tone of the chromatic scale; when this is done certain tones of the chromatic scale are not used. This is due to the fact that the sound of the major scale is achieved only when whole steps occur between all tones of the scale except 3–4, and 7–8, where half steps occur.

5. The *natural minor* scale is heard when the syllables for any major scale are sung beginning and ending on *la.* Since the half steps fall between different steps, the minor does not sound the same as the major scale.

fourth grade upward

Notation for Pitch

The Grand Staff (Key of C)

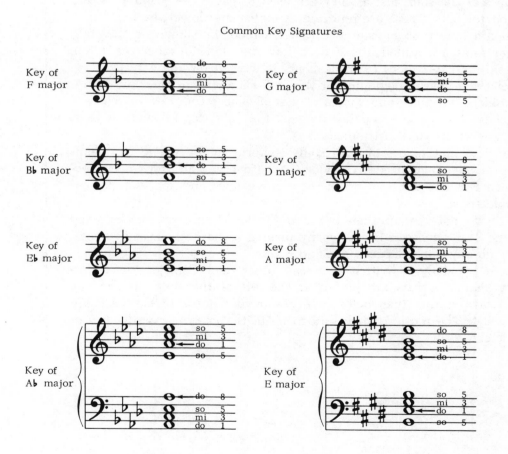

Common Key Signatures

Key of
F major

Key of
G major

Key of
B♭ major

Key of
D major

Key of
E♭ major

Key of
A major

Key of
A♭ major

Key of
E major

6. A minor scale has more harmonic strength when the seventh step of the scale is raised (then called the *leading tone*). Raising this tone creates another form of the minor scale, the *harmonic minor*.
7. The harmonic minor scale can be made in another way: by beginning on the first tone of the major scale and flatting each third and each sixth scale step.

sixth grade upward

E. Notation for Pitch

1. The pitch of musical tone, referred to as high or low, is shown as high or low on a music *staff*. Each step of a scale is represented by the consecutive lines and spaces of the staff. (See diagram on Page 53.)
2. The first seven letters of the alphabet are used to name the lines and spaces of the staff, just as they are used to name the piano keys and resonator bars. These are repeated at higher and lower levels.

third grade upward

3. When a tone is so high or low that it cannot be shown on the staff, *leger lines* are added above or below the staff to show the pitch. Music for bass voices or instruments is written on another staff.
4. A clef sign at the beginning of the staff shows what tones are represented by the lines and spaces of a staff. The *treble clef* (G clef) is used for high voices and instruments; the *bass clef* (F clef) is used for low voices and instruments.
5. The lines and spaces of both staffs conform to the whole- and half-step arrangement of the C-major scale; that is, half steps occur between E-F and B-C; all other consecutive lines and spaces represent whole steps.
6. To write notes other than those in the scale of C major, half-step changes of pitch can be shown by placing a sharp or a flat as necessary on any line or space, before the note.
7. When a melody is written in a scale other than C major, the necessary sharps or flats are placed at the left of the staff (as the *key signature*) rather than before every note that needs to have a sharp or a flat. The music is then said to be in the *key of F* or the *key of G*, etc.

fourth grade upward

chapter 9   Harmony and Texture in Music

Variety in texture

Chords and their relationships

Seeing and building chords

Since so many teaching aids are available today, boys and girls can arrive at an elementary understanding of harmony by the end of the sixth grade. Particularly useful are the many kinds of recorded music and the special classroom instruments, such as resonator bells and the autoharp. Concepts of harmony can be introduced when children learn to play the autoharp and sing with it; as early as the second or third grade, children can hear the difference between the tonic and the dominant chords. Later they can sing rounds that represent a different texture in music. Listening to music offers still more opportunities for studies in musical harmony and texture.

Within the generalizations given on the following pages, all of the items in the first two groups could be understood by children without reference to music notation. It is important that these effects first be pointed out as they are heard. Later, children should see the notation for the particular effect.

It is only in the fifth and sixth grades that children begin to build chords and use their understanding of melody as the basis for an introduction to some of the specifics of the system of harmony. The desire to play chord accompaniments on resonator bells and on the piano can lead to an understanding of all the items listed under "Seeing and Building Chords" (also see Swanson, pp. 128–138).

Although some items are explained, the following outline is not a study of harmony—it is merely a listing of the musical properties that children can find meaningful. These concepts should be introduced through musical examples; they do not need to be studied in depth in these grades. In your handbook, you may wish to break them into smaller segments, depending upon the grade you teach and the repertoire you use to bring the ideas to the attention of the children.

As a teacher you will need a good understanding of all these aspects of music. Listening and participating in activities in the music education class will help. However, you should broaden your understanding by listening to recommended musical compositions and by studying some of the following books: Boyden, pp. 42–52; Copland, Chapters 6, 8; Ratner, pp. 41–68.

A. Variety in Texture

1. When some kind of chord accompaniment supports one main melody the effect is called *harmony*. (In advanced study, this is called *homophonic texture*.) } *first grade upward*

2. When a melody is harmonized, the harmony may have different qualities of texture: slow-moving chords that are held while the melody moves through several tones; chords that are played on almost every note of the melody; chords that are broken and played in arpeggios, or repeated accompaniment figures.

3. Two or more melodies of equal importance sounding at the same time create *counterpoint*. The *round* and *canon* are simple types of counterpoint. (In more advanced study, this is called *polyphonic texture*.) } *third grade upward*

4. An accompaniment that consists of a rhythmic-melodic pattern repeated over and over is called an *ostinato*.

5. Sometimes two or more voices within a composition move for a shorter or longer time in *parallel motion*. The intervals between the voices usually are thirds or sixths, which are sweet-sounding, *consonant intervals*. This kind of harmony is found in two-part songs for children's voices and between the upper parts of "barbershop quartet" arrangements. } *fourth grade upward*

6. Sometimes two parts within a composition move in opposite directions, or in *contrary motion;* a *descant* is often set in contrary motion to the melody.

B. Chords and Their Relationships

1. A chord is a group of tones sounded together. The *tonic chord* (I) is the "home" chord and gives the feeling of restfulness and arrival. Musical compositions often begin with tonic-chord harmony and usually end on it. } *second grade upward*

2. The *dominant chord* (V) is an active, restless chord; its tones tend to move to tones in other chords, usually the tonic.

3. The *subdominant chord* (IV) is called the "amen" chord because its smooth, pleasant sound is heard as the first chord in the "amen" at the end of a hymn. } *third grade upward*

4. The tonic chord (I), the dominant chord (V), and the subdominant chord (IV) are the three chords most used in simple harmonies of hymns and folk music. All of these are bright-sounding *major chords* when a major scale is used. } *fourth grade upward*

5. When a melody is harmonized, chords that fit with its important tones must be used. Some tones that are short or that do not occur on accented beats in the melody can be treated as *passing tones* or *neighboring tones,* which are not harmonized.

6. When a minor scale is used the tonic chord (I) and the subdominant chord (IV) are *minor chords;* such chords have a sweet, pleasant sound that is darker in quality than that of major chords.

7. When the harmony moves from the dominant chord to the tonic chord at the end of a piece, it creates a feeling of arrival and finality (later identified as a *full cadence*).

]— *fourth grade upward*

8. When the harmony moves from subdominant (IV) to tonic (I), the result is a less strong "amen" cadence (later identified as a *plagal cadence*).

9. Sometimes a phrase or larger section of a composition ends on tones of the dominant chord; this is a very temporary kind of ending (later identified as a *half cadence*).

10. In a major key the *supertonic chord* (II) is a minor chord, and it sometimes is used to provide a quality of sound that contrasts with the major chords.

]— *fifth grade upward*

11. Some chords in modern music produce tense, clashing sounds that are called *dissonant.* The composer uses dissonance to create effect and feeling in his music; it is not necessarily unpleasant.

12. Composers of modern music sometimes use chords from two different keys at the same time (*polytonality*). Such combinations of tone create variety and interesting musical effects, although they may seem dissonant and jarring to those accustomed to more traditional harmonies.

]— *sixth grade upward*

C. Seeing and Building Chords

1. The simplest chord, a *triad,* consists of three tones built up in thirds from any step of a scale. The tone on which a chord is built is called its *root.*

]— *fourth grade upward*

The Basic Chords

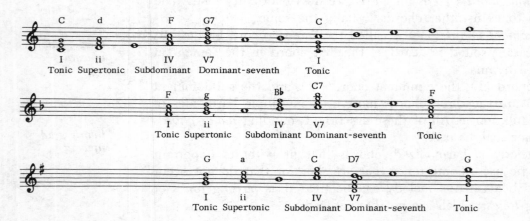

2. Chords are labeled in three ways: with a Roman numeral, indicating the scale step on which the chord is built; with a capital letter (as seen on the autoharp) showing the letter name of the note on which the chord is built; or by a name indicating its harmonic function—i.e., *tonic* (I) or *dominant* (V).

        fourth grade upward

3. The dominant-seventh chord (V₇) has four tones and is used instead of the dominant (V) when a richer, more dynamic quality is desired. (This is the form of the chord available on the autoharp.) The dominant-seventh is a major chord with an added third on top, which is an interval of a seventh from the root of the chord; this is a dissonant chord that forces the harmony to move.

        fifth grade upward

4. Some chords having the same letter name and formation are found in different keys. The function and harmonic effect of a chord depend upon its relationship to the *tonal center* of the key in which it is used, just as each tone of the scale has its own relationship to the key tone.

5. A chord can have some tones doubled, or it can be inverted and still retain its general characteristics and function.

        sixth grade upward

chapter 10   Tone Color in Voices and Instruments

Vocal tone

The strings

The woodwinds

The brass

The percussion

Tone color (timbre) in music can be explored and studied in the elementary school in a number of ways. When tone is the center of a study of instruments and voices it is necessary that the children have an opportunity to play the instruments and to hear them in performance, either live or recorded. The first experiences and observations come in the kindergarten and primary grades, where children hear differences in singing voices and where they explore the tone quality of various classroom instruments. By the time they have completed the sixth grade, children should be acquainted with the tone quality of most instruments and voices; they should have some understanding of the importance of tone color as an element of music (see Swanson, pp. 78, 243–247).

This chapter deals only with the essential characteristics of tone quality of the different voices and instruments. To get an idea of the scope and importance of this subject to a composer, read Copland, Chapter 7. Further information on instruments and voices can be found in Stringham, pp. 207–240, and Walton.

A. Vocal Tone

1. Some voices are higher than others; the voice of a child or a woman is usually much higher than the voice of a man.
2. A voice can be soft and gentle, or loud and brilliant, or exciting, depending upon the feeling that is to be conveyed in the song. (This list of adjectives identifying vocal expression should be expanded in successive grades.)

first grade upward

3. Voices of different people have different qualities of sound; some voices have a smooth, velvety sound, others may sound rough or nasal, or dark and veiled. (Other adjectives can be used to describe vocal tone quality as children hear a greater variety of voices in successive grades.)

second grade upward

4. When people sing together under the direction of a leader, they may be singing in a *chorus* or a *choir*. Most singing groups in church, or those that sing sacred music, are called choirs. (Later, as children hear different singing groups, they can learn what voice parts make up a children's choir and an adult chorus or choir, and that an a cappella choir is unaccompanied.)

third grade upward

5. Girls, some women, and boys with unchanged voices are classified as *sopranos*. Such a voice is high, light, and bright in quality.
6. Women with lower, darker, or heavier singing voices are classified as *altos*. Some children who sing lower tones better than upper tones take the lower (alto) part in two-part music.

fourth grade upward

7. The highest and brightest man's voice is the *tenor;* a man's voice that sounds four or five tones lower and is deeper and more somber in quality is called a *bass*.
8. When people sing together in small groups, with each voice on a different part, they may sing in a duet, a trio, a quartet, or a sextette. ("Barbershop" quartets and famous ensembles from opera or oratorio can be heard.)

fifth grade upward

9. Among highly trained singers, voices are classified according to musical expression and the dramatic roles played. The voice of the *coloratura soprano* is brilliant and agile with a very high range; the *lyric soprano* voice, sweeter and lighter in quality, is given more quiet roles in opera than those sung by the heavier voice of the *dramatic soprano*.
10. The quality of voices among men singers is likewise varied. There are *lyric, heroic,* and *robust* tenor voices; each voice reflects to some extent the qualities associated with the name. The *baritone* is the full, middle-range male voice, and the *basso profondo* is the deep, powerful male voice often playing the solemn role of a king or priest in opera.

sixth grade upward

B. The Strings

1. A musical tone is made on some instruments when a tightly stretched string is plucked with the finger, set in vibration by a bow drawn across it, or struck by a small felt hammer. (In successive grades, children can become further acquainted with the plucked or strummed instruments, such as the *guitar, ukulele, banjo, autoharp, psaltery, zither,* and the *harp;* they should learn to differentiate between the tones of the bowed stringed instruments and the keyboard instruments.)

2. Strings that are long and thick produce heavy, low tones of long duration; strings that are short and very thin produce high, bright tones of shorter duration. (In successive grades, the concept of *pitch* is related to high- and low-sounding strings on different instruments; children learn how strings are stopped by the fingers at higher or lower positions on plucked or bowed instruments to make higher or lower tones.)

3. All stringed instruments have a sounding board or a resonating body that vibrates when the string is sounded, reinforcing the tone so it is loud enough to be heard. (Children touch different instruments to feel the vibrations created; later they learn how the player controls the *volume* of the tone by various playing techniques.)

4. On many stringed instruments the *duration* of the tone depends upon the length of time the string continues to vibrate after it has been struck or plucked; the violin and other bowed instruments can produce a singing tone because the player can use the bow to draw a smooth, continuous tone. (In successive grades, children can hear how the bow is used on instruments of the violin family to create very short, dry tones called *staccato;* long, connected tones called *legato;* or light, lifted tones called *spiccato.*)

5. The piano has the widest *range* of tones from low to high; it has a different string (usually double or triple) for each pitch. The harp's strings are similar to the piano, but it is played by plucking the strings with the fingers rather than by striking them with a hammer, as on the piano. (Later, children can learn to recognize such musical effects as *glissandos, arpeggios,* and running *scale passages* on both instruments, and uses of the pedals of the piano.)

first grade upward

6. Among the bowed stringed instruments, the *violin* is the highest in pitch and tonally the most versatile; its tones can be soft and lyric, soulful, or dramatic and exciting. The *viola,* which is a little larger, has a darker, more sonorous tone. The *cello,* not so agile or brilliant in tone as the violin, can sound dramatic, robust, or tender and soulful. The *double-bass* has the lowest and most powerful tones of this group of instruments.

fourth grade upward

7. The harpsichord looks like a grand piano, but its tone is produced by a mechanical plucking of the strings with leather plectrums. The tone, although limited in dynamic range, is crisp and sparkling; the harpsichord is considered the ideal keyboard instrument for much music by Bach, Handel, and other composers of the baroque period.

8. The bowed strings make up half of the symphony orchestra, providing the basic tone quality for that group. There are some orchestras with nothing but strings.

9. The string quartet is an ideal small group because the tones of the instruments blend to form a well-balanced musical ensemble. The quartet consists of first violin, second violin, viola, and cello. Their parts are comparable to soprano, alto, tenor, and bass in vocal groups.

fifth grade upward

C. The Woodwinds

1. A musical tone is made on some instruments when a person blows across a hole in a short pipe, as across a bottle; the *flute* and its half-sized relative, the *piccolo*, are played this way. The higher tones of the flute can be very bright and penetrating, but the lower tones may sound hollow and dark. (In successive grades, children can learn more about playing the flute and its tone quality; they can compare it with the *recorder*, an end-blown flute with a soft, more intimate tone quality.)

2. In all woodwinds, the tone is raised or lowered by opening or closing holes down the length of the instrument. Since the mechanism that closes the holes lies conveniently under the fingers of the player, he can play very rapidly, leaping from low to high tones easily. (Later, children can learn the different musical effects of legato and staccato played on these instruments.)

second grade upward

3. Some wind instruments are played by blowing through a *single-reed* mouthpiece at the end of the instrument. The *clarinet* is the most important of this group; its tone is rich and full, but quite bright on the high notes. (Later, children can learn to know the different qualities of the clarinet in its three registers; they can become acquainted with the rich, low tones of the *bass clarinet* and the mellow but sometimes reedy tone of the *saxophone*.)

third grade upward

4. Other wind instruments are played by forcing the breath through a *double reed* (flattened "soda-straw" type) mouthpiece. Of this group the *oboe* is well known. It is about the size of a clarinet, but it has a relatively unchanging tone that is somewhat nasal and sometimes pastoral or oriental in quality.

5. The bassoon is a larger double-reed instrument; it has a wide dynamic range and such tonal versatility, from grandiose to plaintive or humorous, that it sometimes is called the clown of the orchestra. (In successive grades, children can become acquainted with the plaintive,

fourth grade upward

reedy tone of the *English horn* and the heavy, somber tones of the *contra-bassoon*.)   ⌐ *fourth grade upward*

6. The woodwind instruments are important "color" instruments in the symphony orchestra because their tones contrast well with the string tone, but they can also carry the melody line or provide modest fill-in parts for the whole ensemble. Concert or marching bands, which seldom use strings, depend upon the many woodwind instruments to set the basic tone quality.   ⌐ *fifth grade upward*

D. The Brass

1. The most brilliant, commanding tone of any instrument comes from the *trumpet*. This instrument evolved from the *bugle* which, being limited to only five tones, is used for signaling, e.g., reveille and taps. Because it has three valves, the trumpet can sound any tone and carry a melody beautifully. (At a later time, children learn that the *cornet* is similar to the trumpet, but slightly shorter and less brilliant.)

2. One of the largest instruments of the orchestra is the *tuba*. It is an armful of wound brass tubing with a flaring bell. Because its tone is so heavy and slow-moving, the tuba is used primarily to support the bass rather than to carry melody. (Later, children can learn that the *sousaphone* is a tuba wound so it can be carried on the player's shoulders in a marching band.)

second grade upward

3. A characteristic common to brass instruments is the cup-shaped mouthpiece. The lips of the player produce the tonal vibrations; the tubing and bell amplify the tones; the size and shape of both mouthpiece and the instrument itself determine tone quality.

4. The *trombone* is the baritone-bass of the brass family. It uses a sliding cylindrical tube to form different pitches. The tone quality of the trombone is rich and powerful, but more solemn and dignified than the trumpet; it can sound brilliant when played loud.

fourth grade upward

5. The *French horn* is descended from the natural hunting horn; it is circularly wound, has a large flaring bell and, with its three circular valves, can sound all tones of the scale. Its tone, lower than that of the trumpet, is noble and full; sometimes majestic and brassy. It can be muted for an effect of distance or solitude.

6. The trumpet, French horn, trombone, and tuba add body and brilliance to the orchestral sound. These and other brass instruments are used in greater numbers in the band, where they often provide massive effects.

fifth grade upward

E. The Percussion

1. Some drums emit a deep, resonant tone of long duration; other drums have a tone that is short and penetrating, with a dry quality. (In higher   ⌐ *first grade upward*

grades, children can become acquainted with the tone quality of un-
tuned drums such as *tom-toms, bongo* and *conga drums,* and the *snare*
and *bass drums* of the symphony orchestra. They learn that the size
of the drum, type of material in the drumhead, and the method of
beating all are factors contributing to the different tone qualities.)

2. Some single-toned percussion instruments produce short, dry sounds,
and others produce ringing sounds of longer duration. (Later, children learn to recognize subtle differences in the tones of instruments
such as the *claves, castanets, woodblock, maracas, triangle, sleighbells,
cymbals,* and *gong.* They observe how different qualities of sound can
be produced through different uses of the instruments.)

3. Some percussion instruments are tuned, and melodies can be played
on them. *Glockenspiels, bells,* and *resonator bars* have a bright, bell-
like tone; the tone of the *xylophone* is dry, and it can be either brittle
or muffled, depending upon the type of mallets used. (Later, children
learn that pitch in these instruments is related to the length of the tone
bar or size of the bell.)

*first grade
upward*

4. There are two kinds of drums in a symphony orchestra: tuned drums
and those of indefinite pitch. Both the *snare drum* and the *bass drum*
are of indefinite pitch. The *kettledrums (tympani)* are tuned drums
with the shape of large copper kettles. A symphony orchestra usually
has two or three tuned to different pitches; the tone is deep, resonant,
and important to majestic or triumphant expression by the orchestra.

5. Many single-toned percussion instruments, such as *castanets, triangle,
cymbals,* and *gong,* are used in the symphony orchestra for special
effects. The xylophone and glockenspiel are used occasionally.

6. Among the tuned instruments with bell-like tones is the *celesta,* which
is essentially a glockenspiel attached to a keyboard (it looks like a
small piano). Its tone is very delicate, with little carrying power. The
orchestra chimes, tuned metal tubes, are struck with a wooden hammer
to produce a tone of great resonance and duration.

*fifth grade
upward*

chapter 11   Form and Design in Music

The phrase as a unit of musical form

Sectional forms of music

Non-sectional forms of music

Suites and dramatic forms

Form has been characterized as the intellectual aspect of music because the mind must remember and compare the use of rhythmic, melodic, and harmonic elements heard at one point with their development and continued use throughout the composition. While the comprehension of form in large works like symphonies requires skill and experience in music listening, many aspects of form and design in music are well within the understanding of elementary school children.

The study of musical form begins early, as children expand their singing repertoire. At that time they use and observe melodic motives and phrases that are basic units in musical design; they learn how phrases are put together and how a melodic motive can be developed and varied in small ways. Concepts about such fundamental aspects of form are outlined in the first section of this chapter. It is only after children understand some of the techniques a composer can use to create variations on one theme that they are ready to undertake a study of the larger forms in music.

The entire activities program in music offers opportunities for observation and use of principles of musical form (see Swanson, pp. 59–60, 92–96, 200–202, 235–242).

The aspects of form in music within the grasp of elementary pupils are listed on the following pages. You should study these carefully, and then consider how they can be taught within the repertoire of songs and recorded instrumental music in the activities sections of your teaching handbook. Those concepts that are not exemplified within the repertoire suitable for your class should be delayed for consideration at a later time.

If you need a better understanding of musical form you can find explanations and examples in Boyden, pp. 33–35, 55–64; Copland, Chapters 10, 11, 12, 14, 15, 17; Ratner, pp. 68–73, 176–188, 248–264.

A. The Phrase as a Unit of Musical Form

1. Music is built up of phrases and sections that, together, make up the whole composition.
2. A song or other short piece of music usually consists of several well defined phrases, some alike and some different.

first grade upward

3. Often there is an even number of phrases in a composition, but sometimes the number is uneven.
4. Within one composition, the phrases usually are the same length, but sometimes a phrase is longer or shorter than others.
5. A phrase can be repeated exactly (A, A); it can be repeated, but with some changes (A, A'); or it can be followed by another that is in contrast to it (A, B).

second grade upward

6. Sometimes two phrases sound like question-and-answer within a longer musical unit. (Later these are identified as *antecedent* and *consequent phrases* within a musical *period*.)
7. Some phrases give the impression of a long flowing line, but others readily divide into short melodic motives.

third grade upward

8. A phrase may be composed of one important motive that is repeated and expanded, or it may consist of two or more different motives.

fourth grade upward

B. Sectional Forms of Music

1. Some songs and short instrumental pieces seem perfectly symmetrical and balanced, because a second section completes or answers the first section; songs having a stanza followed by a refrain, and some marches and dances, have this form. (Later this may be called *two-part or binary form* and shown as A, B in analysis.)

third grade upward

2. A musical composition may have a very satisfying first section that is followed by a contrasting second section. When the first section is repeated at the end, the whole piece seems well balanced and complete. Some cradle songs, waltzes, minuets, preludes, and other short pieces are written in this form. (Later this may be called *three-part or ternary form* and shown as A, B, A in analysis.)
3. Sometimes a first section is alternated with two or more other sections. Since the first section comes 'round after each different section is played this form is called a *rondo*. The rondo usually is lively and cheerful in nature. (Later the rondo form may be diagrammed as A, B, A, C, A, etc.)

fourth grade upward

4. A composer can use any arrangement of sections that is suitable to his musical material. Some compositions that are clearly divisible into sections do not fit any of the prescribed plans. (Later these can be called *free sectional* form and analyzed as A, B, B; A, B, C, A; etc.)

fifth grade upward

5. Sometimes a composer selects a short song or dance (or composes an original one) and writes a series of *variations* on it. Each section is the same length as the original melody, but each is treated in a different way:

    (a) the theme may be ornamented; passing tones, turns, and other decorations can be added to the melody or the accompaniment;

    (b) the theme may have a change in its basic rhythm, melody, or mode;

    (c) the accompaniment may be altered by a change in rhythm, harmony, tone color, or dynamics.

    fifth grade upward

6. Two large sectional forms in music are the *sonata* and the *symphony*. The sonata is written for a solo instrument (e.g., piano alone, or violin with piano accompaniment), and the symphony is written for full orchestra. These large forms consist of three or four related but separate *movements*. A single movement might be a three-part form, a rondo, a theme with variations, or a *sonata-allegro form*. In the sonata-allegro form, usually the first movement in a symphony, the composer contrasts and develops his themes in some generally prescribed ways. (More specific consideration of these large developmental forms are undertaken by students at the secondary level.)

    sixth grade upward

C. Non-Sectional Forms of Music

1. Sometimes a melody in one voice (vocal or instrumental part) is followed by successive voices that enter separately, imitating the first voice throughout. The different voices, singing in *counterpoint* to one another, overlap any phrase endings so that the whole seems to be one continuous composition. (This can be identified as a *canon*, of which one form is the *round*.)

2. A short composition may sound unified and unbroken if the composer has used a single pattern of rhythmic movement and textual treatment throughout. (Bach composed some well-known preludes on continuous broken-chord patterns.)

    fourth grade upward

3. One or two musical motives can be so skillfully handled by the composer that they grow into one small unified composition, with no repetitions or contrasting sections. (Debussy composed some piano preludes in this way.)

4. When a composer uses a story or other descriptive idea as the basis for a composition, he may choose not to follow a prescribed design in his music. He may compose the piece in a single movement so that he has greater freedom to develop musical continuity and feeling that express the programmatic ideas. (*Tone poems* often are written in such a *free form*.)

    fifth grade upward

5. In another kind of continuous, imitative counterpoint, a composer may present a *theme* in a single voice (A) which is imitated in turn by

    sixth grade upward

two or three other voices; however, when one voice (A) turns the main theme over to another (B), it then carries a *counter-theme* until the main theme moves on to the third voice (C); then the first voice (A) has a *free* part (non-imitative) until the main theme again returns to it (A). (These can be identified as important characteristics of a *fugue*.)

sixth grade upward

D. Suites and Dramatic Forms

1. Many composers have written music based on episodes and stories to be portrayed in ballet. When the music offers listening pleasure without the dancing, the composer may arrange its strongest parts into a *ballet suite* of contrasting movements for concert orchestra.
2. Any collection of related musical compositions might be a suite. The *classic dance suite,* a popular musical form at the time of Bach, consists of a group of contrasting dances such as the sarabande, minuet, and gigue. In more recent times, composers have written *descriptive suites* that might be called musical pictures of one subject.
3. Almost every motion picture film is accompanied by background music that often contributes to the ideas and feelings conveyed by the film. Later, a composer may arrange an *orchestral suite* from the film music. In earlier times, *incidental music* written for plays was arranged into a suite for separate concert performances.
4. When drama, stage sets, costumes, singing, orchestral music, and dancing are all combined, the impressive stage production is called *opera.* Opera includes music for solo voices and ensembles, chorus, and orchestra to create dramatic effects while portraying a story. The main musical themes of an opera often are introduced in the *overture,* which the orchestra plays before the curtain rises.

fourth grade upward

5. When a large dramatic work is based on a contemplative or religious subject, it may be performed as a concert without costumes, stage sets, or drama. In such music, called an *oratorio,* solo voices and ensembles, chorus and orchestra, and sometimes a narrator are used.

fifth grade upward

chapter 12   Style in Music

Style is the result of particular ways of using the various elements of music and procedures of composition. Each period in history has brought developments of compositional techniques. Always, the composer's use of rhythm, melody, tone color, and harmony has been influenced to some extent by the social and artistic attitudes of his day. The term "style" can be used in different contexts; for general purposes in elementary music education, we consider the broad style periods that have produced music with certain notable characteristics.

Several basic music series for elementary schools include study units about famous composers; there is need for some historical and biographical information of the type provided in these books. In addition, children must be helped to build a musical frame of reference for the varied styles of music they hear. The chief concern of elementary music education is to establish an idea of the sound characteristic of each period. This process begins in the primary grades when children hear music by composers of different styles. Gradually, as they grow to recognize characteristic uses of rhythm, melody, harmony, tone color, and form, children in the fifth and sixth grades find that they can begin to identify the music of different composers.

The earlier style periods are easily defined, but as we move into the twentieth century we encounter a variety of trends in musical composition. For the purposes of elementary music education impressionism can be identified as a style, and subsequent works can be considered together as contemporary music.

Some music of the twentieth century represents the machine age and its impersonal outlook on life. In other music, contemporary composers show their interest in the native music of people everywhere, by incorporating the tunes, rhythms, and harmonies of folk music in their compositions. However, within this body of diverse musical composition, general characteristics unique to this age can be identified.

This chapter lists the important characteristics of each period, naming representative composers. Although children of all grades should hear music of the various styles, they will not be ready to make comparisons of style until the fifth or sixth grade.

The graded books in the basic music series will help you in the important task of selecting music by the composers listed that will be appropriate for your grade. Other resources are: Swanson, pp. 38–39, 51–52, 64, 221–222 and 230–242; Boyden, pp. 161–167, 200–207, 223–228, 276–297 and 376–388; Ratner, Chapters 5 and 6 and pp. 223–304; Stringham, pp. 165–171, 265–299; 419–445 and 518–563; Copland, Chapter 16. Educational records of the Bowmar Orchestral Library *and R.C.A. Victor's* Adventures in Music *will also be helpful.*

A. The Baroque Style

1. Baroque music has a strong, steady rhythm, and a firm bass line. The treble voice is somewhat florid, using distinctive figurations and embellishments of the melody.
2. A baroque composition features a single theme that is extended, elaborated, and intensively explored. The variation form and the fugue lend themselves to such treatment.
3. Instrumental music of the baroque period features alternation of solo and larger groupings of instruments.
4. Baroque composers liked to give a vivid representation of words, ideas, and feelings in the music itself.

Composers:
Bach, Lully, Couperin, Handel, Corelli, Vivaldi.

B. The Viennese Classic Style

1. Melodies of the classic composers have some qualities of folk songs and dances of that day; they have a simple expressiveness and clear-cut beauty of line.
2. Regular metric groupings provided the rhythmic basis for classic music. The effect of clear, well-balanced phrases, periods, and larger sections is characteristic of the style.
3. Music of the classic period makes ingenious use of motives and themes that are set in contrast to one another, elaborated and developed throughout an entire section of the work.
4. The predominant effect of classic music is homophonic—that is, one melodic line stands out. However, melodic material is shared by instruments of the ensemble; there is skillful use of counterpoint that is subsidiary to the leading voice.

Composers:
Haydn, Mozart, Grétry, Beethoven (early works).

C. The Romantic Style

1. The large orchestral piece of one grand, unbroken movement is characteristic of the romantic style; picturesque episodes within the composition suggest different aspects of an idea or event.
2. Instrumental tone color is used to convey feeling and effect in this music; e.g., massive, rich, low-pitched sound may provide heroic effects, and unusual combinations of high and low may be used for brilliant contrasts and flashes of color.

3. Chromatic tones, indefinite cadences, and some irregularity of rhythmic flow contribute to a mood or pictorial image. Chords are used for their color effects and emotional qualities; certain complex, dissonant chords create rich enchanting sound as well as strong movement in music.

4. Groups of short pieces in different moods, written for solo voice or instrument, especially the piano, are characteristic of the romantic style.

Composers:

Berlioz, Verdi, Schubert, Schumann, Wagner, Tchaikovsky, Mendelssohn, Chopin.

D. The Impressionist Style

1. Melodies in this style tend to seem vague; they consist of short motives rather than long singing lines.

2. Rhythms of the impressionist style often have a vague pulse, and are obscured by syncopation. Subtle use is made of dynamic changes.

3. Chords are used for their color value and sonority rather than for the dynamic quality of movement. When sectional forms are used, the outlines are blurred.

4. Tone color in impressionist music is rich but subdued, pastel, and misty. The harp is frequently heard; many instruments are muted; piano solos use much pedal to sustain and mix chord colors and tonal outlines.

Composers:

Debussy, Delius, Griffes, Ravel, Respighi.

E. Contemporary Music

1. Rhythm is energetic and driving in music of the twentieth century. Often it seems erratic. Sometimes there is no regular duple or triple grouping of beats; accents seem shifted or misplaced.

2. Melodies in contemporary music tend to be jagged and fragmentary. Sometimes folk tunes and motives are used, but seldom in long, flowing lines.

3. Contemporary harmony can be dissonant and clashing. Much use is made of counterpoint, and it, too, may produce dissonance. Opposing musical lines may be written in different scales; different sections of the orchestra may play chords simultaneously in different keys.

4. Contemporary music often shows sectional forms. Phrases can be heard in a question-and-answer relationship. Sections may end with an abrupt shift to a different harmony or texture rather than with a cadence.

Composers:

Copland, Bartók, Honegger, Thomson, Kodály, Milhaud, Harris, Prokofiev, Villa-Lobos, Menotti, Shostakovich, Britten, Stravinsky, Kabalevsky, Vaughn-Williams.

Appendix

Songs for Musical Experience and Analysis

SUMMER IS A-COMING IN

(Sumer is i-cumen in)

Old English
Canon for Treble Voices
14th Century

Lively duple meter

Sum - mer is a - com - ing in,_____ Loud - ly sing cuc - koo!
Sum - er is i - cum - en in,_____ Lhu - de sing cuc - cu!

Grow - eth seed and blow - eth mead, And spring - eth wood a - new.
Grow - eth sed and blow - eth med, And spring - eth w - de nu.

Sing cuc - koo! Ewe_____ bleat - eth af - ter lamb, Low'th
Sing cuc - cu! Aw - e ble - teth af - ter lombe, Lhouth

af - ter calf the cow; Bul - lock start - eth, buck, too, vert - eth,
af - ter cal - ve cu; Bul - luc ster - teth, buck - e ver - teht,

Mer - ry sing cuc - koo! Cuc - koo, cuc - koo!_____
Mur - ie sing cuc - cu! Cuc - cu, cuc - cu!_____

Well sing'st thou, cuc - koo!_____ O cease thee nev - er now!
Wel singes thu, cuc - cu!_____ Ne swik thu na - ver nu!

MY HEART EVER FAITHFUL

(Aria from Cantata No. 68)

J. S. Bach

Presto

This is an excerpt from a longer aria (measures 1–15 and 51–52). Transposed from the Key of F; translated from the German.

joice,_____ sing prais-es____ your__ Je - sus is here!

PAPAGENO'S MAGIC BELL SONG

(from Finale to Act I, The Magic Flute)

Mozart

It__
Das__

ring-eth   so   glo-ri-ous,   it__   ring-eth   so   fair!   La - la-
klin-get   so   herr-lich,   das__   klin-get   so   schön!   *La - la-*

Transposed from the Key of G. Play small notes in refrain 2nd time only.

ra,   la la   la-ra-la, la   la   la-ra-la.   Ne'er
ra,   la la   la-ra-la, la   la   la-ra-la.   Nie_

have I   its   like-ness e'er heard   and be-held!   La-ra-
hab' ich so   et-was   ge-'hört   und ge-seh'n!   La-ra-

la   la la, La-ra-la la la, la-ra-la.   Ne'er   la.
la   la la, La-ra-la la la, la-ra-la.   Nie   la.

WHITHER?

("Wohin?" from the song cycle, "Die schöne Müllerin")

Franz Schubert

This is an excerpt of the 1st 5 phrases from a longer song. Transposed from the Key of G; translated from the German.

CRADLE SONG
(Wiegenlied)

Johannes Brahms

With gentle motion

Lul-la - by and good - night, with_ ro - ses o'er-
Gu-ten A - bend, gut Nacht, mit_ Ro - sen be-

spread,_ slip_ in - to thy_ bed there_ pil - low thy
dacht,_ mit_ Näg - lein be - steckt schlupf_ un - ter die

head. If God will thou shalt wake when the morn - ing doth
Deck. Mor - gen früh, wenn Gott will, wirst du wie - der ge-

break, if God will thou shalt wake when the morn ing doth break.
weckt, mor - gen früh, wenn Gott will, wirst du wie - der ge - weckt.

Transposed from the Key of E This song is also found in GROWING WITH MUSIC, *Book Five*, p. 19 (GwM V-19).

SHADOW MARCH

Alec Rowley
Words by R. L. Stevenson

Mysteriously

All round the house is the jet - black night; It stares thro' the win - dow pane; It crawls in the cor - ners, hid - ing from the light, And it moves with the mov - ing flame. Now

From *Voices of the World*, NEW TOGETHER-WE-SING Series, published by the Follett Publishing Company, Chicago, Illinois. (Foll VI-22.)

my lit - tle heart goes a - beat - ing like a drum, With the

breath of the bo - gey in my hair; And all round the can - dle the

crook - ed shad-ows come And go march - ing a - long up the stair. The

shad - ow of the bal - us - ters, the shad - ow of the lamp, The

shad - ow   of   the   child   that   goes   to   bed_____

All   the   wick - ed   shad - ows   com - ing   tramp,   tramp,   tramp,_____

With   the   black   night   o - ver

head.

100th PSALM

From the Ainsworth Psalter
Amsterdam, 1612

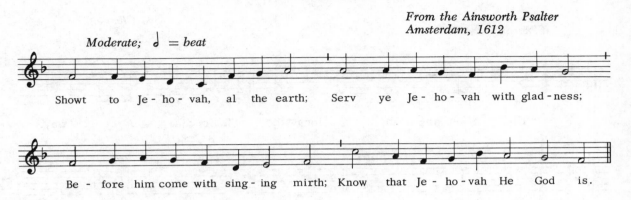

Moderate; ♩ = *beat*

Showt to Je - ho - vah, al the earth; Serv ye Je - ho - vah with glad - ness;

Be - fore him come with sing - ing mirth; Know that Je - ho - vah He God is.

THE SHEEPSHEARING

English Folk Song

Legato

How de - light - ful to see, in these eve - nings in spring,

The___ sheep go - ing home to the fold.___

The___ mas - ter shall sing, as he views ev - 'ry - thing,

And his dog goes be — fore him where

told,___

And his dog goes be - fore him where told.___

From *100 English Folk Songs* edited by C. Sharp, © 1916 the Oliver Ditson Co. Used by permission.

SHENANDOAH

Sea Chantey

Slow and sustained

Oh, Shen-an-doah, I long to hear you, A - way, you roll-ing riv-er. Oh, Shen-an-doah, I long to hear you, A - way, I'm bound a - way, 'Cross the wide Mis - sou - ri.

From *Music in Our Country,* © 1956, Silver Burdett Company.

THE BELL DOTH TOLL

Three-Part Round

Stately

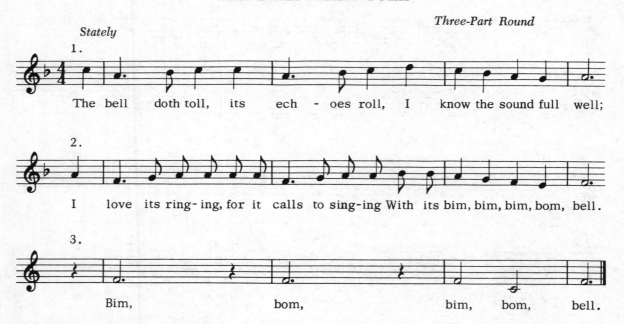

1. The bell doth toll, its ech - oes roll, I know the sound full well;

2. I love its ring-ing, for it calls to sing-ing With its bim, bim, bim, bom, bell.

3. Bim,   bom,   bim, bom, bell.

From *Singing in Harmony* of OUR SINGING WORLD Series, Copyright 1951 by Ginn and Company. Used with permission. (Ginn VI-199.)

ALOHA OE

Queen Liliuokalani
English version by Stephen Fay

CARMEN, CARMELA

Mexican Folk Song
English version by Mabel Livingstone

M'SIEU BAINJO

Louisiana Folk Song
Adapted by Max T. Krone

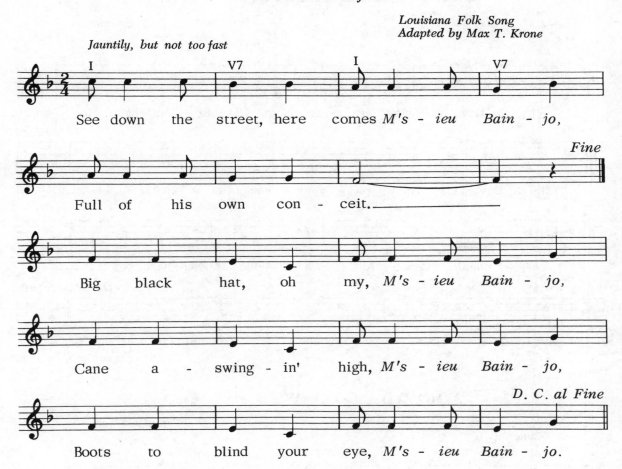

Jauntily, but not too fast

See down the street, here comes M's - ieu Bain - jo,

Full of his own con - ceit.

Big black hat, oh my, M's - ieu Bain - jo,

Cane a - swing - in' high, M's - ieu Bain - jo,

Boots to blind your eye, M's - ieu Bain - jo.

GOOD-BY OLD PAINT

Cowboy Song

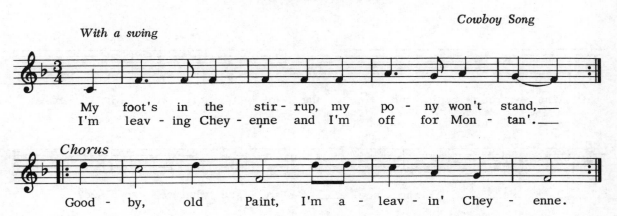

With a swing

My foot's in the stir - rup, my po - ny won't stand,___
I'm leav - ing Chey - enne and I'm off for Mon - tan'.___

Chorus

Good - by, old Paint, I'm a - leav - in' Chey - enne.

From *Voices of America* of the New TOGETHER-WE-SING Series, published by the Follett
Publishing Co., Chicago, Illinois. (Foll V-52.)

LITTLE DAVID PLAY ON YOUR HARP

Spiritual

Lively

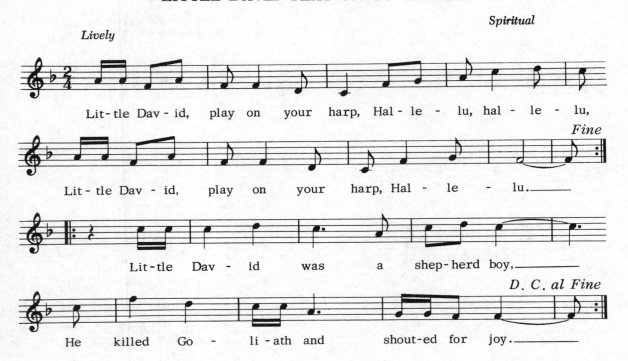

Lit-tle Dav - id, play on your harp, Hal - le - lu, hal - le - lu,

Fine

Lit-tle Dav - id, play on your harp, Hal - le - lu._____

Lit-tle Dav - id was a shep-herd boy,_____

D. C. al Fine

He killed Go - li -ath and shout-ed for joy._____

WHO WILL COME WITH ME?

Traditional Song

Gaily

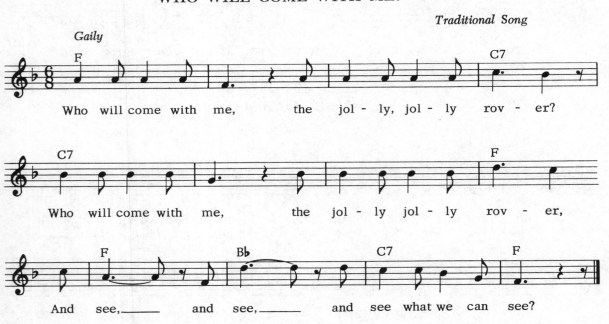

Who will come with me, the jol - ly, jol - ly rov - er?

Who will come with me, the jol - ly jol - ly rov - er,

And see,_____ and see,_____ and see what we can see?

From *The Singing Circle* by Lady Bell. Used by permission of Mary Lady Trevelyan and
Longmans, Green & Company, Limited.

THE GREEN DRESS

South African Song
Josef Marais

Gaily

When - ev - er Het - ty puts a green dress on,

green dress on, green dress on,

When - ev - er Het - ty puts a green dress on

I will sing a song for her.

Let us sing a song, it need - n't be so long,

My Het - ty has a green dress on. on.

AH, LOVELY MEADOWS

(Aj, lúčka, lúčka široká)

Czech Folk Song

In March Tempo

Ah, love-ly mead-ows, green and wide, Grass-es are grow-ing, grass-es are grow-ing Ah, love-ly mead-ows, green and wide, Grow-ing— so high on ev-'ry side. (Hey!)

Chorus

Wa-ter from moun-tain flows, Melt-ed from win-ter snows, Turn-ing, it gai-ly goes, Cir-cling the ma-ple tree— Wa-ter from moun-tain flows, Melt-ed from win-ter snows, Turn-ing, it gai-ly goes, Call-ing to me. (Hey!)

From *Music Highways and Byways,* © 1936, Silver Burdett Company. (NMH VI-168.)

SHOO, FLY

Singing Game

Lively

Shoo, fly, don't both - er me, Shoo, fly, don't both - er me,

Fine

Shoo, fly, don't both - er me, For I be - long to some - bod - y.

I feel, I feel, I feel, I feel like a morn - ing star,

D. C. al Fine

I feel, I feel, I feel, I feel like a morn - ing star. So

Also found in MAKING MUSIC YOUR OWN Series, *Book Two*, p. 82. (MM II-82.)

Bibliography

Andrews, Gladys. *Creative Rhythmic Movement for Children*. Englewood Cliffs, N.J.: Prentice-Hall, Inc., 1954.

Bergethon, Bjornar, and Eunice Boardman. *Musical Growth in the Elementary School*. New York: Holt, Rinehart & Winston, Inc., 1963.

Boyden, David D. *An Introduction to Music*. New York: Alfred A. Knopf, Inc., 1956.

Broudy, Harry S. "Educational Theory and the Music Curriculum," *Music Educators Journal*, November-December 1964.

Coleman, Satis N. *Creative Music for Children*. New York: G. P. Putnam's Sons, 1929.

Copland, Aaron. *What to Listen for in Music*, Rev. Ed. New York: Mc-Graw-Hill Book Co., Inc., 1957.

Dykema, Peter W., and Hannah M. Cundiff. *School Music Handbook*, New Ed. Evanston, Ill.: Summy-Birchard Publishing Co., 1955.

Edman, Irwin. *Arts and the Man, A Short Introduction to Aesthetics*. New York: W. W. Norton & Company, Inc., 1939.

Elliott, Raymond. *Teaching Music: Methods and Materials for the Elementary Schools*. Columbus, Ohio: Charles E. Merrill Books, Inc., 1960.

Fox, Lillian Mohr, and Thomas L. Hopkins. *Creative School Music*. Morristown, N.J.: Silver Burdett Co., 1936.

Hartshorn, William. "The Role of Listening," Chapter 11 from *Basic Concepts in Music Education*, 57th Yearbook of the National Society for the Study of Education, edited by Nelson B. Henry. Chicago: University of Chicago Press, 1958.

Jones, Archie N., ed. *Music Education in Action*. Boston: Allyn and Bacon, Inc., 1960.

McMillan, L. Eileen. *Guiding Children's Growth Through Music*. Boston: Ginn and Co., 1959.

Mursell, James L. (I) *Music and the Classroom Teacher*. Morristown, N.J.: Silver Burdett Co., 1951.

——————— (II) *Music Education Principles and Programs*. Morristown, N.J.: Silver Burdett Co., 1956.

Myers, Louise Kifer. *Teaching Children Music in the Elementary School*, 3rd Ed. Englewood Cliffs, N.J.: Prentice-Hall, Inc., 1961.

Nye, Robert Evans, and Vernice Trousdale Nye. *Music in the Elementary School,* 2nd Ed. Englewood Cliffs, N.J.: Prentice-Hall, Inc., 1964.

Orff, Carl, and Gunild Keetman. *Music for Children, I—Pentatonic.* English adaptation by Doreen Hall and Arnold Walter. Mainz, Germany: B. Schott's Söhne, 1956; Associated Music Publishers, Inc., N.Y.

—————. *Music for Children* (recording). Angel Records 3582B.

Pitts, Lilla Belle, et al. *The Kindergarten Book.* OUR SINGING WORLD Series. Boston: Ginn and Co., 1959.

Ratner, Leonard G. *Music—The Listener's Art.* New York: McGraw-Hill Book Co., Inc., 1957.

Schubert, Inez, and Lucille Wood. *The Craft of Music Teaching.* Morristown, N.J.: Silver Burdett Co., 1964.

Seeger, Ruth. *American Folk Songs for Children.* New York: Doubleday & Co., Inc., 1948.

Sheehy, Emma D. *Children Discover Music and Dance.* New York: Henry Holt & Co., Inc., 1959.

Stringham, Edwin John. *Listening to Music Creatively,* 2nd Ed. Englewood Cliffs, N.J.: Prentice-Hall, Inc., 1959.

Swanson, Bessie R. *Music in the Education of Children,* 2nd Ed. Belmont, California: Wadsworth Publishing Co., Inc., 1964.

Taylor, Katherine Scott. "An Autochthonous Approach to Music Appreciation," *Music Educators Journal,* February-March, 1949.

Tooze, Ruth, and Beatrice Perham Krone. *Literature and Music as Resources for Social Studies.* Englewood Cliffs, N.J.: Prentice-Hall, Inc., 1955.

Walton, Charles W. *Instruments of the Orchestra, A Teaching Guide.* RCA Victor record album LE/LES 6000. Camden, N.J.: Radio Corporation of America, 1962.